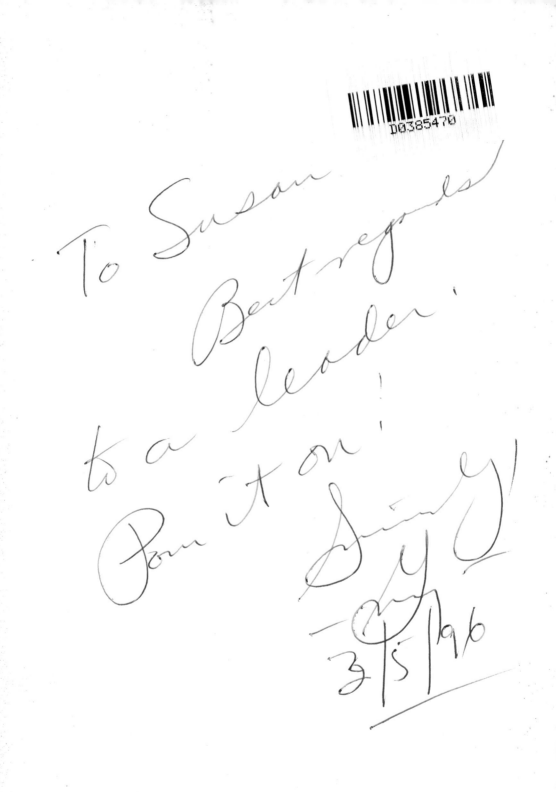

To Susan

Best regards

to a leader.

Pass it on!

Sincerely

3/5/96

What Leaders in the Insurance Industry Say about *Secrets of Successful Insurance Sales* **and Its Authors:**

"An excellent book about success, both in selling insurance and in life. A refreshing affirmation of key principles that many of the most respected agents I know use as the foundation of their business success."

Arch Cassidy
Agency Manager, The Equitable

"Secrets of Successful Insurance Sales is a masterpiece by none other than the masters themselves, Jack and Garry Kinder and W. Clement Stone."

J.J. Miller, FSA, CLU
Sr. Vice President, CMO,
Western-Southern

"After a score of years in the field where they 'lead by example,' and years of preaching that which they practiced, the Kinders and W. Clement Stone share their greatest secrets in this, their finest text."

Gary Schulte, CLU
Sr. Vice President, CMO, Executive Life

"Jack and Garry Kinder, along with W. Clement Stone, have a unique way of expressing their secrets. It all leads to a better you in selling."

Cal Roebuck
Regional Vice President, State Farm

"Much of the success that our agency has had is due to the sound techniques and philosophies of Jack and Garry Kinder."

Burr Anderson, CLU
General Manager, New York Life

"The thing that always impresses me most about Jack and Garry Kinder is that they speak from experience and everything they say has a practical application. The ideas you, as an agent, will discover in this book will have a fantastic, positive impact on your selling career."

Jim Richardson
Sr. Vice President, AAL

"It is a lot easier to sell life insurance by benefitting from the knowledge and experience of other successful producers.

"Your book, *Secrets of Successful Insurance Sales,* has helped me now, after twenty years in the business. It certainly would have helped me as a new agent entering the life insurance business."

Frank Caliri, Sr.
Insurance Broker

"Not only does this book offer solid and specific information in the usual Kinder style, but it introduces the 'value added' approach . . . just what our industry needs right now."

Bill Campbell, CLU
Vice President, Farm Bureau Insurance

"This is a book that could not possibly fail to help even the most seasoned professional—not to mention its value to the novice. Again, Jack and Garry Kinder, along with W. Clement Stone have focused on the fundamentals that make the difference in successful selling."

Mike McAdams, CLU
General Agent, Mass Mutual

". . . Excellent . . . stepping stones to enjoying a superlative sales career. Regardless of your level of experience, your sales career will be enhanced utilizing the messages taught in this great book."

Eugene C. Sorrel
Director, National Marketing
Colonial Life

"The unique combination of the Kinder brothers and W. Clement Stone will make this book a 'must' for all people in our industry. These three men are truly giants in the life insurance profession."
Ted Santon, CLU
Chairman, Lincoln Financial

"During the past 10 years, I have seen first-hand the power of the Kinder/Stone philosophy generate enthusiasm for our business. Their 'secrets' have literally created and increased production in our agency."
W. Jay Carey, CLU
General Agent, The New England

"The Kinders do it again . . . an excellent book that focuses on staying 'brilliant on the basics.' Timely!"
Ken Martin, ChFC
President, First Protective

"I'm on my third reading. If the response I've received so far from the people who asked about it on the plane, at the workshops I've been doing, and even here in the home office is any indication . . . you have an all-time best seller."
Bill Wetzel, RHU
Vice President, Protective

"The Kinders have shared many of their 'secrets' with me over the years. Their assistance has provided motivation and inspiration, and spurred our success. Anyone in the life insurance business will benefit from the advice given here."
Gary L. Kaltenbach, CLU
General Agent, John Hancock

"Like the true mentors that they are, the Kinders and W. Clement Stone continue to lead the way when it comes to helping agents 'climb the ladder.' This book will be a valuable 'road map' throughout your career."
K. Wayne Townsend, B.A., CLU,
London Life

"*Secrets of Successful Insurance Sales* gives an agent the power needed to become successful today and remain successful throughout a career."

Ron Price
Vice President, Agency
Iowa Farm Bureau

"Having personally relied on the counsel and advice of Jack and Garry Kinder for the last twelve years, I would strongly recommend this book for any producer wanting to add power to their sales career."

David B. Bell, Jr., CLU
President, First Protective

"The distance from hearing how, to knowing why, is usually a long and bumpy road. In their new book, *Secrets of Successful Insurance Sales,* Jack and Garry Kinder make it as easy as a trip along the Milky Way."

Frederick J. Jarosz, LUTCF
Executive Vice President, CMO
The Horace Mann Companies

The PMA Book Series
W. Clement Stone, General Editor
Robert C. Anderson, Editorial Consultant

This series of books presents practical approaches to achieving success and fulfillment in business, professional, and personal life.

Based on the proposition that there is an intelligent solution to every human problem and that with a positive mental attitude (PMA) a person can overcome any adversity, each book in this series offers practical, step-by-step advice and inspiration to action.

Titles in this Series Include:
Jerry Baker's Growth Plan for People, Jerry Baker
Believe and Achieve: W. Clement Stone's New Success Formula, Samuel A. Cypert
Secrets of Successful Insurance Sales: How to Master the "Value Added" Approach to Consultative Sales, Jack Kinder, Jr., Garry Kinder, and the Napoleon Hill Foundation
Earl Nightingale's Greatest Discovery: The Strangest Secret . . . Revisited, Earl Nightingale

Upon request, the owner of this book will receive an autographed bookplate bearing the signatures of the authors. Address your request to the Napoleon Hill Foundation, 1440 Paddock Drive, Northbrook, IL 60062, enclosing a large (business-size), self-addressed, stamped envelope. With the bookplate you will receive a copy of one of Napoleon Hill's famous success essays.

Secrets of Successful Insurance Sales

HOW TO MASTER
THE "VALUE ADDED" APPROACH
TO CONSULTATIVE SALES

JACK KINDER JR.
GARRY KINDER
AND THE NAPOLEON HILL FOUNDATION

With Motivational Commentaries by W. Clement Stone

W. Clement Stone
PMA Communications, Inc.
Northbrook, IL 60062

Published by W. Clement Stone PMA Communications, Inc.
1440 Paddock Dr, Northbrook, IL 60062
Manufactured in the United States of America
Second Edition

1 2 3 4 5 6 7 8 9 10

Library of Congress Cataloging-in-Publication Data

Kinder, Jack, 1928–
  Secrets of successful insurance sales.

  (The PMA book series)
  Bibliography: p.
  Includes index.
    1. Insurance—Agents. 2. Selling. I. Kinder,
Garry D., 1933–   II. Napoleon Hill Foundation.
III. Title. IV. Series.
HG8876.K56 1988   368′.068′8   88-16178
ISBN 0-396-09329-9

Contents

Foreword

Many books are published each year on the subject of selling, but only once in a great while does one of them merit wide circulation. It's my opinion that *Secrets of Successful Insurance Sales* is one of those rare exceptions. The authors are phenomenally successful personalities in the insurance field. Jack and Garry Kinder are well-known throughout the industry for their platform skills and consulting strategies. W. Clement Stone developed a sales system that made top producers of all who learned it and were inspired by his Positive Mental Attitude (PMA) philosophy.

The product of life insurance is a contract for time and money. Most prospects want to feel more secure about both. The agent who can help prospects attain this security will be successful. This book is a practical guide to such success. Its illustrations are easy to grasp and apply, its abundant exercises are calculated to assist you in "interactive" learning. Throughout, it demonstrates the need for focus on the client. It teaches "consultative selling," how to become "client focused" rather than "product driven."

I know of only two ways in which money can be made in the insurance field—they are an individual at work or money at work. This book shows you how to use both methods. Although its emphasis is on individual efforts and techniques, it does not neglect the latest dimension that has been added to the insurance agent's role, that of financial adviser.

Read the book, digest it, and come back to it often to rework the exercises and reabsorb its principles. If you do, your dream of being a high achiever in sales of life insurance is assured.

—Ben Feldman, CLU

Introduction

This book grew out of the discovery, in 1986, of an unpublished manuscript by Napoleon Hill, author of *Think and Grow Rich*. Michael J. Ritt, Jr., executive director of the Napoleon Hill Foundation in Northbrook, Illinois, knew that sometime during the 1950s Hill had written a book entitled *The Science of Successful Insurance Selling*, but the work had been lost among the trunks full of papers left by the author at his death in 1970.

Hill had organized the text as a series of seventeen lessons, apparently to be taught in a seminar context, each lesson based on one of the Seventeen Principles of Success that he and W. Clement Stone developed when they worked together on seminars and books, including the self-help classic *Success Through a Positive Mental Attitude*.

Ritt was elated with his find. He knew that the insurance-industry examples and figures were too outdated to make the book viable as it stood, yet it would be a shame to let the old master's views on insurance sales languish forever in a dusty archive box. So he sought W. Clement Stone's advice on what to do with it.

In July 1986, Stone sent the manuscript to the editorial office of PMA Books with a four-page memo that began, "There are some excellent ideas in this book. However, a lot of changes are necessary." It went on to detail changes that should be made to update the text, and concluded with the suggestion that I find some outstanding life-insurance salesperson who could write a book using some of the Hill material.

As it happened, I knew *two* authorities who might want to tackle such a project: the Kinder brothers. I'd had a lot of favorable reports on their consulting work in the past, and I'd sat in on their seminars and written an article about them for *Success* magazine. So I contacted the Kinders about the project and discovered that, coincidentally, they were about to embark on writing a new book on insurance sales.

The Kinders jumped at the opportunity to work with W. Clement Stone, and before you could say "PMA," we had a deal.

As the great Ben Feldman, (He's much more than another great name) says in his foreword, this book makes use of the wisdom of the past in explaining the latest approaches in selling.

The Kinders believe that after thirty years of slow but dramatic changes—changes in product, nonmedical limits, binding authority, the level of sophistication of prospects and their ability to purchase substantial amounts of insurance when they are persuaded to do so—the insurance industry has arrived at a Golden Age.

This new era abounds with opportunity, but it demands a very high level of professionalism on the part of the agents, who must be able to diagnose and creatively solve client problems in order to make sales. The Kinders refer to this buyer-oriented approach as "*need* selling rather than *greed* selling." They teach what they call a "value-added" approach to selling.

Briefly summarized, *value-added* means that the agent

- keeps up with developments in the industry and is well informed on current events and trends in business
- is perceptive about clients' needs and responsive to changes in clients' situations
- is able to personalize and tailor recommendations to the particular client
- is organized to follow up on sales and provide prompt, accurate, and courteous continuing service
- is sensitive to client moods, feelings, and personal opinions in dealing with them
- displays conscientiousness and professionalism at all times, especially when working with clients.

There was another consideration that made the Kinder brothers ideal as authors of this work: part of their early training in the field was attending the original PMA Science of Success lectures given by W. Clement Stone and Napoleon Hill in Chicago. So, integrating Hill's seventeen lessons with their own modern sales techniques was a labor of love for the Kinders.

The result is a book that delivers a payload of professional insurance-sales techniques for space age use with a guidance system formed of the strongest and most practical attributes of Napoleon Hill's philosophy. It ignores Hill's less pragmatic ideas, some of which, such as his views on sex and religion, have been controversial.

For readers unfamiliar with Hill, his interest in the philosophy of success began when, as a young journalist, he interviewed the great industrialist Andrew Carnegie, who said to him, "Isn't it a shame that men spend their entire lives accumulating knowledge through the trial-and-error method, and at a point in life when one is just about at his height in wisdom, death strikes him down, and his storehouse of knowledge, all of his know-how of success, goes to the grave.

"I am looking for a man whom I can commission to assemble this know-how of success through years and years of research into a written philosophy," Carnegie continued. "I want future generations to profit by it without having to learn through the difficult lifetime process of trial and error."

Hill volunteered to undertake that assignment, and he spent twenty years doing the research and interviewing outlined by Carnegie. The result was the publication, in 1928, of *Law of Success*, followed in 1937 by *Think and Grow Rich*.

The principles of success developed by Hill and later refined by him and W. Clement Stone into the PMA Science of Success are central to the structure of this book. They are most apparent in the first chapter (Hill's first principle was Definite Major Purpose), but they are evident throughout.

Thus, in more than incidental fashion, this book is based upon generations of experience dating back to Andrew Carnegie. So, in addition to its prescriptive lessons, this book bears more than a lifetime of substance for future reference and thoughtful reflection. We are proud to include it in the PMA Series.

— Robert C. Anderson
Editorial Consultant
The PMA Book Series

Secrets of Successful
Insurance Sales

Commentary: PMA and Your Life's Goals

When you can answer the question, "What is my big goal in life?" you are already well on your way to success. For as I have told audiences around the world, definiteness of purpose combined with PMA (Positive Mental Attitude) is the cornerstone and starting point of all worthwhile achievement.

In the early sixties President John F. Kennedy told us that Americans would walk on the moon by the end of the decade. Neither he nor NASA knew how they would get there. But once the goal was established and given a deadline, the energy and scientific understanding of the nation focused on achieving it. What had seemed impossible became reality in July of 1969, when Neil Armstrong and Edwin Aldrin landed their Apollo 11 Lunar Module on the moon.

Make the Principle Work for You

The same principle that brought success to the national goal of putting men on the moon applies to your personal goals. When you know what your big goal is, several good things happen: First, your subconscious goes to work, following the universal law that "What the mind can conceive and believe, it can achieve." Because you visualize your intended destination, your subconscious is affected by this self-suggestion and seeks ideas and solutions to help you get there. Second, because you know what you want, you recognize opportunities that will help you attain it. You get on track. You get into ACTION! Third, work becomes fun. You are motivated to pay the price. You budget your time and money. You study, think, and plan. The more you think about your goal, the more enthusiastic you become. And with enthusiasm, your desire turns into a *burning desire*.

I assume, since you are reading this book, that your big goal involves becoming a top producer in the field of insurance sales. Congratulations! As one who started his own agency with one hundred dollars and built it into what is now the multibillion-dollar Aon Corporation, I know what a thrill it is to wrestle with the challenges of our great industry and win.

You Can Be a Winner, Too

Your success is assured if you study the ideas in this book. Get involved with them. Think them through for yourself and visualize how you can apply them in the specific circumstances you encounter. Underline key words and phrases as you read. This will help you remember them and will serve as a guide when you need to refresh your recollection of certain concepts. Underlining also helps you recognize trigger words that can be used to motivate yourself and others. You can use such words and phrases deliberately as self-motivators, and I suggest that you begin developing the habit of doing so now. Being able to use self-motivators will help you keep your mind on your goal despite distractions, and help you direct your thoughts and energies in a positive way. Here's how it works:

One of my favorite self-motivators is the phrase, *"Do it now!"* which I use to overcome procrastination. I employ the method of self-suggestion, which French psychologist Dr. Emil Coué developed in the 1920s. Coué discovered that he could cause spontaneous remissions of disease in some patients and even prevent illness by having patients repeat over and over as they were going to sleep or awakening the phrase, "Every day in every way, I'm getting better and better." I extended the technique to overcome a tendency to procrastinate by repeating the phrase *"Do it now!, Do it now!, Do it now!"* This engraved the phrase on my subconscious so that whenever I was tempted to think, "Oh, that can wait. I'll do it later," the phrase, *"Do it now!"* would flash into my mind. This is called auto-suggestion, and I always immediately reinforce it when it occurs with ACTION. For instance, if I'm getting ready to leave a room and a pen falls to the floor, the temptation is to leave it there. I can pick it up later (or the cleaning lady will). But *"Do it now!"* flashes into my mind, and I pick up the pen. I do not want to lose the habit of responding to the autosuggestion.

You can do the same with *"Do it now!"* or any of the self-motivators you'll find at the end of each chapter of this book. For you are a mind with a body, and your brain and nervous system comprise the most powerful device that this universe has ever known—a human computer. The electronic computer was designed to function like your human computer, but even the biggest and most powerful of the electronic computers is primitive compared with the one you possess.

I suggest that you program your internal computer by using another motivational technique of mine, the R2A2 Formula. In this formula, R2 stands for Recognize and Relate; A2 stands for Assimilate and Apply. The complete formula is: R2A2—Recognize, Relate, Assimilate, and Apply *principles* from what you see, hear, read, think, and experience, or from other disciplines to attain any worthwhile goal that does not violate the laws of God or the rights of your fellow man.

Use the R2A2 Formula as you read this book (and remember that to *apply* principles means to take ACTION), and your success is guaranteed.

Develop a Positive Mental Attitude

Before you begin reading Chapter 1, let me give you a little coaching on how to develop PMA. You'll get a lot more out of this book if you approach it with a Positive Mental Attitude.

Go to a mirror and look at yourself. Don't be bashful now, tell that good-looking image that's looking back at you, with sincerity and enthusiasm: "I feel HEALTHY, I feel HAPPY, I feel TERRIFIC!" Repeat that several times a day. Whenever anyone asks you how you feel, tell them, "I feel HEALTHY, I feel HAPPY, I feel TERRIFIC!" Soon you will notice that you really do feel healthy, happy, and terrific. Positive action stimulates positive thinking. Moreover, you will find that others begin to respond to you in a positive way. This may be the greatest benefit of all, especially in selling.

—*W. Clement Stone*

Chapter One
The Power of Purpose
Building Correct Attitudes

The greatest discovery of my generation is that people can alter their lives by altering their attitudes of mind. What the mind attends to, it considers. What the mind attends to continually, it believes. And what the mind believes, it eventually gets done.

— William James

The first and most important secret of successful insurance sales is that there are no secrets. That's right — *there are no secrets!*

There are many aspects of the business that may seem to be secrets, especially in the mind of the inexperienced agent. But their mystery is precisely there — in the mind.

To begin to clear away the fog of mystery and see the path to success at your feet, you need only one attribute: the right attitude of mind. And what is the right attitude? W. Clement Stone spells it out in his commentary opening this section, it's what he calls PMA: a Positive Mental Attitude. Here are some of the chief characteristics of PMA:

Optimism — A positive attitude has a hopeful sense of the promise of the future. It acknowledges problems, but it sees them not as obstacles but as opportunities.

Enthusiasm — A positive attitude says "yes" to life. It affirms individuality and encourages others.

Initiative—A positive attitude is action oriented. It constantly seeks knowledge as well as enjoyment of things that are good, true, and beautiful in life and nature.

Faith—A positive attitude affirms God, the values of our Judeo-Christian heritage, and the power of prayer.

These characteristics—optimism, enthusiasm, initiative, and faith—give rise to a pair of potent motivators of human behavior, *desire* and *belief*. And purpose is formed by desire and belief. When a person earnestly desires something and believes it is attainable by him or her, the pursuit of it becomes purpose.

As Hank McCamish, a great agent from Atlanta, once told a Million Dollar Round Table audience: "Radiate the attitude of well-being, of confidence, of a person who knows where he or she is going. You'll find that good things begin happening right away." If you do not have a definite purpose in mind, project the positive attitude Hank McCamish described and you will soon discover one.

Every field of endeavor has many examples that testify to the role of purpose in the achievements of men and women who set the pace for others and become outstanding.

For Terry Fox, the need to settle on a life purpose was thrust upon him at an early age. Two days after his eighteenth birthday, the young Canadian learned that he had a cancerous tumor in his right knee and that his leg would have to be amputated.

Following the operation, as he was enduring painful chemotherapy treatments, and learning to walk on his artificial leg, he realized that he could no longer take his life for granted; time might be running out. Rather than waste that time in self-pity, he resolved to set an immediate goal for himself: he would help mankind by raising a million dollars to fight cancer. He would establish a fund-raising "Marathon of Hope," and he himself would run across Canada, donating the money he raised to the Canadian Cancer Society.

Powered by definiteness of purpose, and running on his artificial leg, Fox managed to complete a marathon every day for five months, going three-fifths of the way across Canada before failing health forced him to abandon his "Marathon of Hope" on September 1, 1981.

Whatever his ultimate goal may have been, he never reached it, for the cancer spread to his lungs, and he died in June of 1982. But he had raised more than twenty-four million dollars, and perhaps even more important, he became an inspiration to thousands of cancer victims. He still is.

Terry Fox symbolized what most of us want to know — that there is purpose to life. Your being here does mean something. What you do as an agent can and does make a difference.

The Power of the Made-up Mind

High achievers in all fields understand the power of the made-up mind. You have heard it said of them, "They think right." *Again, these are the individuals with a settled purpose. They have discovered the power of the made-up mind.*

Dr. Edward Rosenow, a renowned surgeon at Mayo Clinic, established his purpose in life and sealed his commitment to medicine when he was just a small boy living in Minnesota's northwoods country. One night, he says, his younger brother became quite ill, and the family gathered together, waiting nervously until a doctor could be located.

When a doctor finally arrived and examined the sick boy, young Edward's eyes were riveted on the anguished faces of his parents. At last, the doctor looked up, turned to the parents, and said, "You folks can relax now. Your boy is going to be all right." Edward Rosenow, then just eleven, was so impressed with the change the doctor's words brought to his parents' faces, that he said, *"I resolved right then that one day I would become a doctor, so I could spend my life putting that same light in other people's faces."*

There are few experiences more rewarding than putting light in other people's faces. Yet it is a reward that comes often to the insurance agent who becomes thoroughly imbued with the value of the contribution he or she makes when properly selling financial products and services to clients. These are the agents who discover a worthwhile purpose in meeting prospects' needs and satisfying their expectations. They believe in themselves and in their products and in their mission. And because they do, they consistently achieve superior results. *Never underestimate the power of maintaining definiteness of purpose.*

Advantages to You

There are six major benefits to be gained by applying the definiteness-of-purpose principle to your selling life:

1. *Definiteness of purpose reinforces in the person who possesses it the positive-attitude characteristics of self-reliance, personal initiative, imagination, enthusiasm, self-discipline, and concentration of effort.* "Concentration is my motto—first honesty, then industry, then concentration," said Andrew Carnegie.
2. *Definiteness of purpose motivates you to budget your time and to plan day-to-day selling activities.*
3. *Definiteness of purpose makes you more alert in recognizing sales opportunities.* It inspires a sense of urgency to act upon these opportunities.
4. *Definiteness of purpose inspires confidence and attracts the favorable attention of prospects and clients.*
5. *Definiteness of purpose opens the way for that great state of mind known as faith.* Purpose keeps the mind positive and frees it from the limitations of fear and doubt, discouragement, indecision, and procrastination. This is undoubtedly the greatest of its many benefits.
6. *Definiteness of purpose helps you develop and maintain a "burning desire" to achieve.*

The Future Has Never Been Brighter

Economists tell us the immediate future will offer the professional salesperson the greatest rewards in history. He or she works today in an environment salespeople have looked forward to and dreamed of for many years. There are few positions in business today that offer bigger opportunity, more security, and greater satisfaction through serving others than

8

the career of a well-qualified, professional salesperson. He or she not only enjoys high income potential, but can also take a great deal of credit for the high standard of living our population enjoys.

But it's you, the insurance agent, who is favored with the greatest opportunity of all as our country enters this historic high point of its development. Why? Because in today's marketplace, in this rich and informed environment, the average prospect accepts the modern-day life-insurance product as an important purchase and asset. Nevertheless, that average prospect is still only covered for less than three years of spendable income. Each day, fifty-five thousand people die in the United States, two-thirds have no life insurance, and relatively few have a claim for more than fifty-thousand dollars. Yet these same prospects earn incomes higher than ever before. And, as consumers, they find much of that income is discretionary—spent for products and services over and above the basic necessities of food, clothing, shelter, and medical care.

More businesses and more individuals with more dollars to spend and invest offer new and easily accessible avenues to bigger and better sales. These selling opportunities exist for the professional agent who effectively learns to make the call, ask the questions, discover the needs, arouse interest, make the presentation, close the sale, deliver the contract, and service the business.

It's Up to You

It's an overused cliché to say that "nothing happens until a sale is made." But it's true. And it's especially true as it relates to life insurance and financially related products. Today, the agent who sells these kinds of products must be better informed and more creative. He or she must have a strategy for closing sales that don't close themselves.

It will always be somewhat difficult to sell insurance. *People buy what they want; they must be sold the things they need.* This is why the rewards you can earn as an agent are limited only by you. Since you are your own boss, it is up to you to determine the income and the standard of living you want. Economic ups and downs affect you and your business very little, if at all.

Selling financial products and services is a dynamic, fast-changing kind of a job. Yet, there's a large measure of permanence when you learn to do it well. There is no age limit and virtually no capital investment required. No long years of study and apprenticeship are necessary before earnings begin. In fact, early in your career you can enjoy an income usually achieved only by top-level executives in other businesses with long years of experience.

Big success or small success — it's all up to you!

Your Need for Self-Discipline

Years ago, Albert E.N. Gray delivered a meaningful address in which he identified the common denominator of success. His message has been printed, recorded, and distributed throughout the sales world, and it's still required reading in many sales organizations. That's because it is as important and timely today as it was the day he delivered it. The essence of what he said was:

> Success is always achieved by the minority.
> It's achieved by those who form the habit of doing those
> things the mediocre either cannot or will not do.

And there you have it — the common denominator of success. It lies in forming the habit.

Self-discipline is developed when you stop doing what you know you should not do, and start doing what you know you should — whether you like it or not. In this book you will discover ways to discipline yourself to plan, create the selling climate, make more and better sales, monitor your progress, and perform at your best.

Every qualification for success in selling, as well as in living, is acquired by habit. Habit formation and habit alteration are the results of discipline. *Self-discipline is a magical key for engineering success in selling and in living.*

Stay Focused on Results

As an agent, you are measured and rewarded not by the hours you put in, but by what you put into the hours. Making good on your purpose in business and in life is going to boil down to the way in which you invest your time. If you live to be eighty years old, you will have lived only 29,200 days. Each of those days, therefore, is a precious fragment of a gift called time—your time. It only makes sense to use every day well. Today is yours. Use it well.

Del Smith, the highly successful CEO of Evergreen International Aviation, Inc., says it this way: "I've become convinced that time is the most important factor in human existence. What you do with this precious commodity determines the course of your life. Each minute appears only once in all eternity. If not utilized, it's lost forever."

Jack Parr, a well-known sales consultant from Salina, Kansas, expresses it this way: "If you view the subject of time management only in terms of efficiency—only as guidelines for increasing the number of activities you can pack into a day, you have reason to be repelled by it. If you view it in terms of effectiveness—in terms of disciplines for eliminating unnecessary activities from your busy schedule to make way for satisfying, goal-directed activities, time management will be attractive to you." To increase your sales production and income you probably won't need to work any harder—but you may need to work smarter.

One of the most underrated truths about selling is that unusual success follows the agent who identifies the vital factors that make a significant difference in producing results. This agent then focuses attention on those key, vital factors most of the time. That's what Jack Parr means by saying effective. *The effective agent spends time on the high-payoff activities.*

Stay In the Green

To shape the kind of effective approach described by Parr, you'll find it helpful to view your business activities as being either "green" (vital), "yellow" (important), or "red" (tension-relieving).

An agent's green-time activities are calling for appointments and making sales presentations. Yellow time includes planning, prospecting, studying, preparing, dictating, filing, etc. Each of these yellow activities may be necessary and important; however, improving or doing more of them is no guarantee of an improvement in production.

Red-time activities include drinking coffee and having a lengthy discussion of last night's ballgame. It's an extended luncheon with someone who will never be a client. These and others you can think of are tension-relieving activities.

Clearly, you have high-quality time and low-quality time. Green, yellow, and red activities all keep you busy, but they have strikingly different impacts on your "bottom line." *Remember, you are paid for results produced—not for the amount of time you put in.* Never confuse activity with accomplishment.

Make the Most of Your Time

Like most success factors in selling, time management is largely dependent upon attitude. Develop your awareness of time and the manner in which you use it. Again, time is one of the major resources to utilize if you are to achieve outstanding success as an agent.

Make it a practice to ask yourself, "What should I be doing with my time right now? What is it that really needs doing now? Am I staying in the green?" More than anything else, your attitude determines your success in managing time.

Here are some key time-management, attitude-building thoughts to review regularly:

Define the "ideal day." This serves to reinforce discipline; it eliminates decisions on what to do next and ensures the scheduling of key activities.

When you start something, be determined to do it right the first time and bring it to a finish. The old cliché, "If you don't have time to do it right, when will you have time to do it over?" applies today, too. Resist the temptation to leave a job unfinished. It takes more time to refamiliarize yourself with a project than to complete it the first time around.

Become clock-conscious. Set your watch five minutes fast. It will make you time-conscious and keep you punctual.

Keep your written, daily plan visible. It's one good way to rout procrastination.

Place greater emphasis on what you do each day than on how much you do. Stay in the "green."

Learn to control the telephone effectively. This can free as much as an hour a day, which then can be devoted to top priorities. Master the technique of getting a talkative person off the telephone. Advise him or her early in the conversation when you must leave the line. Decide that telephone interruptions can be controlled.

Try standing while you talk on the phone. This uncomfortable position will remind you to keep conversations shorter.

Avoid playing telephone tag. (This is where you call and find your party out or unavailable. You ask to have your call returned but when they call back, they find you unavailable.) There's a simple solution. Always leave a specific time for returning your call or ask when, specifically, your party can be reached.

Carry a list of frequently used telephone numbers. Don't waste time looking up numbers.

Learn the ideal times to schedule sales interviews with certain types of prospects. For example, see the dentist late in the afternoon—the athletic coach early in the day.

Earn a reputation for being busy. Others will show more respect for your time.

Establish deadlines with plans you make. Set time limits for doing certain jobs. You may have an hour to do a job, but don't take that hour for a thirty-minute job.

Schedule breakfast and luncheon appointments. You will discover "working meals" to be time-savers.

Make note-taking a habit. Don't trust your memory to record such items as appointments, activities, details, or ideas. Many successful agents maintain calendar diaries or daily planners to help make this process automatic. Before they turn the page on a day, they record all pertinent information while it's still fresh. This ensures that information won't be lost or that needless time won't be spent trying to retrieve it.

Have your secretary confirm appointments. This saves time by improving your "batting average" on appointments kept.

Be on time for appointments. Expect others to be on time as well.

Make every call count. If you can't make a sale now, determine when you can.

Schedule personal visits to doctors or dentists only when you can be the first patient of the day. Many professionals don't value their patients' time as they do their own.

Keep your schedule flexible. This lets you cope with priorities when they arrive.

Keep your automobile in top condition. You can't earn commissions if you can't get to your prospect.

Become adept at dictating into a portable cassette recorder.

Make the most of your transition time. You can gain a remarkable amount of information and inspiration if you listen to cassettes during your "in-between" time. Turn your automobile into a learning center. Also, invest in a cellular telephone for your car. Roger Staubach tells us it's his single best time-saver.

Beware of perfectionism. If you tend to be a perfectionist, keep in mind that even by your standards you need to do some jobs quickly and be done with them.

Develop your secretary as an assistant. In addition to handling routine correspondence, answering the telephone, and monitoring visitors and appointments, a secretary can be invaluable in anticipating needs and following up on handling details.

Have a place for everything so that you don't waste time looking for lost files and information.

Make use of specialists where you lack experience. This saves time and speeds up your personal development.

Skim books and magazines for ideas. Learn to skip over unnecessary details and omit copy that's only marginally informative. Take a speed-reading course. Retain usable ideas and quotations on three-by-five-inch index cards.

Check to see if available computer programs can be utilized to save you time.

Take advantage of waiting time. Plan ahead to make this time productive.

Generate less paperwork. Throw away nonessential papers once you have read them.

Handle each piece of mail once. Frequently, a reply to letters can be made on the same sheet of correspondence. Save trivia to be handled once a week.

Avoid "friendly visits." Many agents fall into the trap of looking up friends when they should be making calls.

Decide which responsibilities you must be directly involved in and which ones can be delegated. Be sure to delegate effectively. "Dump and run" is generally a time-waster.

Let drop-in visitors know how much time you have for them.

Plan unavailability. Plan a "quiet hour" each day for concentration and creative thinking. It will pay dividends.

Avoid the false economies of overworking and underexercising. Whenever your habits or working and thinking jeopardize your health and energy level, you lose.

Do first things first! Stay focused on those things that produce the desired results.

Time management is a lifetime activity. To become good at it you must have correct attitudes, workable strategies, and most of all, an adequate amount of self-discipline.

How to Stay on Top

Again, selling power originates from developing and maintaining definiteness of purpose. The strength of your purpose determines the attitudes you develop about selling and the habits you develop for spending your time. "Thinking right" will move you to join the agents who get to the top and stay there.

Make these tenets a dominant part of your selling style:

- **BELIEVE** that the modern-day, client-oriented life-insurance contract is the single best instrument for providing a complete and balanced hedge against the twin economic dangers that confront every prospect: the dangers of living too long or dying too soon.
- **BELIEVE** that financial products and services, properly sold, are of considerably more value to your buyer than any commissions you can possibly earn.
- **BELIEVE** that you are your most important customer. You must be sold on your job, your products, and your ability to perform.
- **BELIEVE** that you should set realistically high goals and achieve them on schedule.
- **BELIEVE** that time is money and that learning to manage your time productively will be one of your most profitable achievements.
- **BELIEVE** in the law of averages and in the wisdom of knowing the dollar value of each of your primary activities: the telephone contact, the fact-finding interview, and the closing interview.
- **BELIEVE** that honest, intelligent effort is always rewarded.
- **BELIEVE** that a selling interview is never to be considered a contest between you and the prospect.
- **BELIEVE** that the power of your sales presentation will always lie in its simplicity.
- **BELIEVE** that the product purchase must be "helped along" and is most often made because you guided the prospect's behavior in an effective manner.
- **BELIEVE** that prospects buy financial products and services not so much because they understand the product thoroughly, but because they feel and believe that you, the agent, understand them, their problems, and the things they want to accomplish.
- **BELIEVE** that almost all development is, in fact, self-development—that personal growth is the product of practice, observation, and self-correction.
- **BELIEVE** that staying physically fit is a prerequisite for maintaining a high level of energy.

16

- **BELIEVE** that top producers are ordinary people with an extraordinary determination to make every occasion a great occasion.
- **BELIEVE** that the spiritual always determines the material.
- **BELIEVE** that there is great power in holding a high ideal of your worth as a professional agent. Your image of yourself determines how far you will go in earning money, gaining clients, and achieving influence.

These are the kinds of philosophies you will find possessed by agents who have warranted pride in their accomplishments. Study them, digest them, make them a dominant part of your selling strategy, and you will find yourself among those agents who go to the top and stay there.

The Greatest Miracle

The most acclaimed self-help writer of our time is Og Mandino. Every book he has written belongs in your library. One of his many best-sellers is *The Greatest Miracle in the World*, and one of the greatest miracles, of course, is you—at your best. Turn on your "mentalvision." See yourself at your best. Our bet is that when you're at your best, you are outstanding—unbeatable—maybe even in a league by yourself.

In *The Greatest Miracle in the World*, Og Mandino offers a simple four-step formula for staying at your best most of the time: First, count your blessings; second, proclaim your rarity; third, form the habit of going the extra mile; and fourth, exercise your power of choice wisely.

At your best, you are the greatest miracle in the world. Putting the power of purpose to work in your selling life will keep you that way.

As Thomas Carlyle said: "The person without a purpose is like a ship without a rudder. Have a purpose in life, and having it, throw such strength of mind and muscle into your career as God has given you."

Carlyle also wrote: "An individual with a half-volition goes backwards and forwards, and makes no way even on the smoothest road. An individual with a whole volition advances on the roughest, and will reach his or her purpose, if there be even a little wisdom on it."

17

There is no road to success in sales but through a clear, strong purpose. Nothing can ever take its place. A purpose underlies character, culture, commitment, attainment of every sort.

And it was Napoleon Hill who reminded us: "The starting point of all individual achievement is the adoption of a definite major purpose and a specific plan for its attainment."

Decide upon your purpose. Insist upon it. Force it into your subconscious mind. Let it dominate. See yourself as having attained it. This is the "secret" of success. It's the door to everything you will ever have or be. You are now—and you will become—what you think about most of the time.

Chapter One Flashbacks

1. Purpose is created by _desire_ and _belief_.
2. People buy what they _want_; but they must be sold on those things they _need_.
3. Success is always achieved by the _minority_.
4. Successful agents _form the habit_ of doing things the mediocre either cannot or will not do.
5. _Self_-_discipline_ is the magical key for engineering success in selling and in life.
6. Never underestimate the power of _purpose_. This produces six major benefits:

    a. _____
    _____
    b. _____
    c. _____
    d. _____
    e. _____
    f. _____

7. There are two "green-time" activities: _calling for appointments_ and _making sales presentations_.
8. More than anything else, your _attitude_ determines your success in managing time.
9. Believe that the power in your sales presentation always lies in its _simplicity_.
10. Believe that honest, intelligent _effort_ is always rewarded.

———————————

For answers see page 229.

Self-Motivators to Build Correct Attitudes

W. Clement Stone explains in his commentary at the beginning of this chapter the use of trigger words and phrases—self-motivators—to stimulate yourself to prompt and correct action. Following are some suggestions for self-motivators you can use in building correct attitudes.

Assuming you have written out a clear, concise statement of your purpose (remember, this is the starting point of all worthwhile achievement), you can avoid getting sidetracked by tempting endeavors in other fields by frequently repeating the self-motivator:

My purpose is _____.

A good one to have on call when the temptation that may lead you away from your purpose is pleasure or entertainment is:

Be self-disciplined!

In the same vein, when you get bogged down in low-payoff activities, a good self-motivator is: _____ .

Work smarter!

To avoid procrastination, use the phrase that W. Clement Stone has made a personal trademark: _____ .

Do it now!

Whatever you vividly imagine, ardently desire, sincerely believe, and enthusiastically act upon, must inevitably come to pass!

—William Arthur Ward

Commentary:
The Magic Ingredient
in Planning

The year was 1983. Britain's Sir Geoffry Howe, chancellor of the exchequer, was being interviewed on television's "Good Morning America" and, later, the "Today Show." I was shocked and amazed at his response to such questions as, "Why are governments, international banks, and nations having such serious money problems?" "Why are great American automobile and other large corporations in trouble?" I was aghast as he shrugged his shoulders and responded: "We assumed the trend would continue."

It seemed incomprehensible to me that the chief planners of a great nation would be unaware of cycles.

Many years ago I had a large loan at the American National Bank and Trust Company in Chicago. One day, Paul Raymond, vice-president in charge of loans, telephoned me and said, "Clem, I am sending a book to everyone who has a large loan with us." I laughed and responded, "I can read. What's the name of the book?" He said, "*Cycles*, by Edward R. Dewey and Edwin F. Dakin."

A Great Discovery

Because I had developed the *habit* at an early age to recognize, relate, assimilate, and apply principles from what I read, saw, heard, thought, and experienced, I discovered upon reading that book a missing ingredient in myself on how to predict my future and make a fortune—and not lose it. In addition, I motivated and trained many persons to do likewise. And that's why I now predict that I shall increase my wealth by a few hundred million dollars in the next five years.

You, too, can predict your future and make a fortune if you are willing to study, learn, plan, apply the principles of cycles and trends, and daily engage in creative, positive-thinking time. Og Mandino did. Og has told the world that *Success Through a Positive Mental Attitude*, coauthored by Napoleon Hill and me, motivated him to change his life from miserable failure to phenomenal success. You may be aware that he was editor of *Success Unlimited* Magazine for several years, and that he wrote *The Greatest Salesman in the World*, *The Greatest Miracle in the World*, *The Greatest Secret in the World*, and *The University of Success*.

Og is a wealthy man. Why shouldn't he be? In addition to memorizing the principles of PMA (Positive Mental Attitude), he established the *habit* of applying and living those principles. When I gave him the book *Cycles*, he became so motivated that he sought out Edward R. Dewey and joined forces with him to write the book *Cycles: The Mysterious Forces that Trigger Events*.*

Bring in New Life, New Blood

In *The Success System that Never Fails*, I wrote: ". . . when I see my business leveling off, I use a principle learned from *Cycles*: Start a new trend with new life, new blood, new ideas, new activities." But I added a new dimension: don't abandon the successful formulas of the past that are effective because of new concepts. Why? Successful individuals, corporations, and nations that subsequently fail, do so because they deviate from the attitude and PMA motivational principles that made them successful in the first place.

**For additional information on (1) scientific papers and books on cycles and trends, (2) the Cycles Bulletin, and (3) a list of specific trends and cycles for any period of the past, present, or future, call or write John Burns, Executive Director, or Gertrude Shirk, Editor, The Foundation for the Study of Cycles, 124 South Highland Avenue, Pittsburgh, PA 15206 (412-441-1666).*

I learned something more from *Cycles*: how to accurately evaluate growth trends and leading indicators. Growth is figured by many executives in actual numbers, rather than in percentages. The chairman, president, and chief executive officer, or entrepreneur who develops the *habit* of evaluating with regularity the rate of growth in percentages and interprets leading indicators by proven formulas can increase and prevent the leveling off or decline of sales and profits.

A Major Fallacy

You will note that I have emphasized the word *habit* where it appears in this commentary. One of the fallacies of educational concepts is that "knowledge is power." That's not true. Knowledge is only potential power. The principles need to be *habitually applied*. I sincerely believe that many of the executives heading great American corporations that have become insolvent, and the high international government officials and international bankers who are experiencing what seem to be insolvable serious monetary problems, were aware of cycles and trends. Unfortunately, they failed to apply the magic ingredient of planning, they didn't develop the *habit* of checking and predicting the future with regularity. There is a universal law: you don't always get what you expect unless you *habitually* inspect.

You can evaluate the principles I'm sharing with you here by one standard only: the action you take and the results you achieve.

—*W. Clement Stone*

Chapter Two
The Power of Planning
Setting Up Your Success

Planning encourages disciplined action. Planning is as important as doing. Planning should always take place before doing.
— Reginald Rabjohns, CLU

Improving Your Odds for Success

Throughout our careers, we have been closely allied and identified with the insurance industry. We have sold policies, hired and trained agents, and served as corporate officers and consultants in this great business.

During this time we have been analyzing the causes of agent success and failure. Our experience has taught us that selling success, financial success, and lasting happiness are, in the main, the result of six things:

1. Living one's life in balance
2. Building a healthy self-image
3. Defining and steadfastly pursuing a series of specific, realistically high goals
4. Setting up a mastermind alliance
5. Developing self-discipline and self-management skills
6. Displaying faith and perseverance.

Life doesn't cheat. It doesn't pay in counterfeit coins. It doesn't lock up shop and go home when payday comes. It pays every person exactly what that person has earned. The age-old law that you get what you earn hasn't been suspended.

When you take these truths into your business life and believe in them— when you thoughtfully complete the yearly step-by-step approach to goal setting and action planning described in this chapter—you will have turned a big corner on the high road that will lead you to success throughout your selling career.

Plan to Win

"Cheshire Puss," she began rather timidly . . . "would you tell me,
please, which way I ought to walk from here?"
"It all depends a good deal on where you want to go to,"
said the cat.
"I don't much care where," said Alice.
"Then it doesn't matter which way you walk," said the cat.

So go the memorable lines from *Alice in Wonderland*. Many sales careers go afoul because the agent doesn't know where he or she is going. You must plan your success conscientiously and know where you are going if you are to achieve the success that can be yours. This encourages disciplined activity. *Planning is the first step toward developing a focus on desired results*.

In this chapter, you'll be introduced to a proven process for setting goals and fixing a plan of action. Then you will learn about the most powerful strategy in all of business—the mastermind principle. We believe you'll find this chapter and its contents the springboard for making you a consistently effective agent—this year and every year.

Setting Goals

An agent without goals is like a ship without a captain. The ship may be seaworthy and have the finest equipment, but without a captain to take command and guide it to a designated port, it goes nowhere.

The key is *direction* and *focus*. An individual with specific goals will display determination and drive. As you learned in the opening chapter, your effectiveness and productivity will be greatly multiplied when you have definiteness of purpose. Tunnel vision is good when your target is clearly identified.

Goal setting is the cause, success is the effect. Goals become motivations. As Curt Ladd, the talented Million Dollar Round Table (MDRT) producer from Dallas, says: "Goals that are reduced to writing and are reviewed and measured regularly are never forgotten or modified. When revisited until internalized as habit, these goals never die."

With this understanding of the importance of goal setting, here are four important guidelines to keep in mind:

1. *Your goals must be achievable.* Why push and strive toward a goal when you know it's beyond your reach? Set your goals high, but be sure they are realistic and attainable by pushing yourself to your limits.
2. *Your goals must be believable.* This is closely related to the first point. Goals must reflect realism, not idealism. Goals must be something you are convinced you can reach.
3. *Your goals must be measurable.* Think about your favorite athletic event. Would you still find it interesting if there was no way of keeping score? What makes football exciting is knowing what the score is and how much time is remaining. It's the same with your goals.
4. *Your goals must have deadlines.* Few people know what they want; still fewer know when they want it. Time is your most precious commodity. It can never be replaced. If you are to use your time most productively, you must commit yourself to a plan of action and you must give that plan a deadline for completion.

Thus, the four pillars that will support your goals are: achievability, believability, measurability, and firm deadlines. The great salesman Ben Feldman put it well when he said: "We need goals and deadlines—goals big enough to be exciting and deadlines to make us run."

There are two chief cornerstones that support success: a sharp *focus* on your goals and a *plan of action* to get you there. In this chapter, we will show you how to evaluate yourself and determine what your life dreams are so that you can specify your goals and establish a plan of action to achieve them. Exhibit 2-1 will help you see the difference between well-conceived and poorly defined goals.

Self-Assessment

The first priority on your road to sales success is to evaluate yourself. There is no substitute for being completely knowledgeable about your greatest asset—you!

Before you can determine where you want to go and how and when you want to get there, you must first know where you are starting from. That's why self-assessment is so valuable. It gives you a starting point.

On the following worksheets you will complete a self-assessment in three important areas—business, personal, and financial. This exercise will serve as a mirror with which to view yourself.

The past cannot be undone.
But, as experience is the great teacher,
so it is that they who cannot remember
the past are doomed to repeat it!

Examining Your Dreams

Your true potential lies dormant until aroused by your belief that dreams can be made to come true.

In the self-assessment step, you took an inward look into the person you presently are. You saw much. Now, you will cast a look forward into the human being you can become. You'll see even more.

Earl Nightingale says: "Success is the progressive realization of a worthy ideal." *Focus your attention now on what you believe to be life's worthy ideals for you.*

In order to do so, allow your mind the freedom of dreaming. What are your life's dreams? What do you have visions of achieving? Lewis Carroll

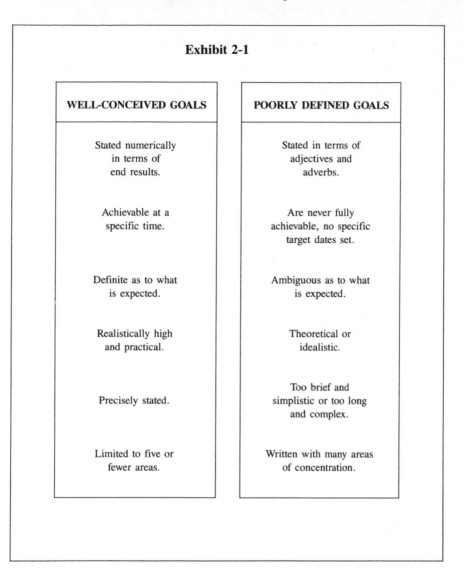

Exhibit 2-1

WELL-CONCEIVED GOALS	POORLY DEFINED GOALS
Stated numerically in terms of end results.	Stated in terms of adjectives and adverbs.
Achievable at a specific time.	Are never fully achievable, no specific target dates set.
Definite as to what is expected.	Ambiguous as to what is expected.
Realistically high and practical.	Theoretical or idealistic.
Precisely stated.	Too brief and simplistic or too long and complex.
Limited to five or fewer areas.	Written with many areas of concentration.

Business Self-Assessment

This proficiency checklist of your skills and abilities is designed to assist you in determining the performance/potential gap in your selling job. Circle the number that represents how well you perform in each category, then add the circled numbers to determine your score.

1. Displaying professional presence   1 2 3 4 5
2. Setting reachable goals with established deadlines   1 2 3 4 5
3. Planning time and activities for the next day   1 2 3 4 5
4. Prospecting in nests   1 2 3 4 5
5. Preapproach effectiveness   1 2 3 4 5
6. Skill in fact-finding and probing   1 2 3 4 5
7. Sales presentation persuasiveness   1 2 3 4 5
8. Meeting objections   1 2 3 4 5
9. Closing skills and strategy   1 2 3 4 5
10. Obtaining referred-lead introductions   1 2 3 4 5
11. Use of weekly reports to determine "dollar value" of each selling activity and progress being made toward my goals   1 2 3 4 5
12. Involvement of specialists in joint selling   1 2 3 4 5
13. Efficient office administration   1 2 3 4 5
14. Use of secretarial, telephone, and mail services   1 2 3 4 5
15. MDRT and NQA qualification, CLU and NALU participation   1 2 3 4 5
16. Staying active in business, civic, and church activities   1 2 3 4 5
17. Reading and cassette listening   1 2 3 4 5
18. Physical-fitness program   1 2 3 4 5
19. Managing personal financial affairs   1 2 3 4 5
20. Personal planned self-improvement program   1 2 3 4 5

Total Possible Score   100
My Score   _____
Performance/Potential Gap In My Sales Job   _____

Personal Self-Assessment

Personal Statistics: Age _____ Height _____ Weight _____

Rate yourself using a scale of 1 to 10 (10 being superior) with respect to your physical, mental, personal, and spiritual attributes:

Physical   _____ Weight-to-height ratio
                  _____ General appearance/posture/smile/dress/hair
                  _____ Exercise/relaxation time
                  _____ Proper nutrition

Date of last physical exam _____

My strongest physical attribute is _____

Physically, I am interested in _____

Mental   _____ Knowledge of selling/people/product
                  _____ Communication skills (speaking/listening)
                  _____ Financial knowledge
                  _____ Knowledge of current events/politics

My strongest mental attribute is _____

I'm confident of _____

I'm committed to _____

Personal   _____ Confidence
                  _____ Family relationship
                  _____ Trustworthiness
                  _____ Financial security

My strongest personal attribute is _____

I feel good when _____

I am excited about _____

Spiritual   _____ Spend time alone every day praying
                  _____ Spiritual goals established
                  _____ Attend church, synagogue, or other religious services
                  _____ Effort spent in developing sensitivity to others

My strongest spiritual attribute is _____

I want to strengthen my life spiritually by _____

I'm grateful for _____

Financial Self-Assessment

Your net worth is your financial mirror image—what you look like on a given day. Just as the looking glass may reveal a surprisingly well-dressed, confident person, so your financial reflection may show a net worth that is growing through savings and investments.

Your net worth is the difference between what you own and what you owe. You will not be able to intelligently establish financial goals until you know your current financial standing.

ASSETS		LIABILITIES	
WHAT YOU OWN		**WHAT YOU OWE**	
CASH:	$ _____	CURRENT BILLS:	$ _____
Cash on hand		Rent	
Checking accounts	_____	Utilities	_____
Savings accounts	_____	Charge accounts	_____
Money-market funds	_____	Credit Cards	_____
Money owed you	_____	Insurance premiums	_____
		Child support	_____
MARKETABLE SECURITIES:		Other bills	_____
Stocks	_____		
Bonds	_____	TAXES:	
Government securities	_____	Federal	_____
Mutual funds	_____	State	_____
Other investments	_____	Local	_____
		Taxes on investments	_____
PERSONAL PROPERTY:		Other	_____
Automobiles	_____		
Household furnishings	_____	MORTGAGES:	
Art, antiques, other collectibles	_____	Homes	_____
Clothing, furs	_____	Other properties	_____
Jewelry	_____		
Other possessions	_____	DEBTS TO INDIVIDUALS:	_____
REAL ESTATE:		LOANS:	
Homes	_____	Auto	_____
Other properties	_____	Education	_____
		Home improvement	_____
		Life insurance	_____
PENSION:		Other	$ _____
Vested portion of company plan	_____		
Vested benefits	_____	TOTAL:	$ _____
IRA	_____		
Keogh	_____	What you own minus what you	
		owe equals your net worth:	$ _____
LONG-TERM ASSETS:			
Equity in business	_____	Net Worth Previous Year	$ _____
Life insurance cash value Annuities	_____		
TOTAL:	$ _____	Net Increase During Year	$ _____

32

said, "It's a poor sort of memory that only works backwards." Project yourself mentally into the future. What would you like to see accomplished in your life?

It's important for a person to dream of what he or she wants to do because, as Georgia Tech's Vice President and Director of Athletics, Homer Rice, says, "People are motivated to do what they themselves decide to do."

On page 34 you will find a worksheet with which you can compile your "Master Dream List."* *Your only limitations are self-imposed.* It's important that you consider everything you want to do, everything you want to learn, everything you want to earn, and yes, everything you want to become.

You make your dreams . . . and then your dreams make you. "The research of neuroscience has proved that what you determine for yourself, what you conceive and give your energies to, will create or call upon a life-force which will turn the dreams you dream into touchable reality." So says Dr. Shad Helmstetter, Ph.D., in his new book, *What to Say When You Talk to Yourself.*

Concise, yet perceptive, is the proverb that states, "Without vision, the people perish."

Establishing This Year's Goals

Motivation occurs when dreams become goals, which, in turn, inspire you to tap unused talent and potential.

High-achievers fantasize, just as we encouraged you to do in the previous step. But they don't stop at dreaming—and neither should you. It's now time to crystallize your objectives. Having established your life's chief aims, you must realign your thinking to the present—to this year. *The future is where you dream; this year is where you live, sell, and perform.*

Yearly goals bridge the gap between where you are presently in selling and where you intend to go. They put you on schedule to achieve your career objectives. Few people know what they want. Still fewer decide when they want it.

A financial budget is a key element in determining your yearly goals. Before you can set intelligent production goals, you must first know what

The Power of Planning

Building My Master Dream List

DREAMS	DATE FOR ACHIEVEMENT
I WANT TO OWN: _____ _____ _____	
I WANT TO KNOW: _____ _____ _____	
I WANT TO DO: _____ _____ _____	
I WANT TO BE: _____ _____ _____	
I WANT TO EARN: _____ _____ _____	
I WANT TO LEARN: _____ _____ _____	

* with acknowledgment to Homer Rice, vice-president and director of Athletics, Georgia Tech University

your financial needs are. A yearly budget will show you the income you must produce—as a minimum.

Money Management

Money management is a critical element in your success as an agent. Your career does not require a large financial investment to get started. You don't need to buy furniture and fixtures, finance an inventory, or construct a building.

Is money management less important to you than to other people who are entering business for themselves? No! As with any independent business, the real financial rewards are in the future. While you build your business, your income may be limited. You will have months of higher earnings and months of lower earnings. *Your ability to manage your personal finances through both is critical to your success*. That's why you have a personal obligation to yourself and to your family to see that your business is well managed.

Often it seems as though increased income would solve all of our money problems. Perhaps it can, but this is not usually the case. A reporter once asked John D. Rockefeller when he would realize that he had enough money. Mr. Rockefeller replied, "When I have a few million more." *Our "wants" have a unique ability to expand in direct proportion to our income*. The effective management of money is a matter of making choices between "needs" and "wants" and decisions about what is most important to you.

Planning your expenses in advance can help point you and your family to financial security and can give you satisfaction and peace of mind. The plan for spending we recommend shouldn't be viewed as a limiting factor. In fact, one of the main advantages of being a commissioned agent is that you don't have to live on a fixed salary. There is unlimited opportunity for incentive. You can earn more than the president of your company, and several agents do.

Debt

You should set goals for yourself and give yourself rewards for a job well done. However, don't give yourself the "reward" before you have earned it! Don't borrow the money to give yourself the reward and then scramble to pay it back. For one thing, it's more expensive. For another, it can lead to financial worries that will hinder your progress as an agent.

For most agents, being in debt is a de-motivating influence.

Contingency reserve

Most people in business experience seasonal fluctuations in their income. They must budget income from peak periods to bridge nonproductive periods and cover expenses. You will experience similar fluctuations in your income for two reasons: (1) fluctuations due to your varying sales success from month to month, and (2) fluctuations due to the premium-payment methods of your clients.

For this reason you should establish a contingency reserve by setting aside funds from peak periods to cover your planned spending needs. Put this fund in a special savings account or special reserve checking account to be drawn on to meet planned spending needs in the event that your monthly income should slip below the planned amount. *This fund should equal twelve to eighteen months' planned spending needs.* While it may take time to build this reserve, now is the time to begin. Begin setting aside dollars from your commission earnings now. This reserve should not be a part of your planned savings program or your savings for a vacation, television set, or new car.

Income taxes

Since you are a business person, the IRS allows you to deduct certain business expenses when documented. Your weekly planner should provide space to record such business-related expenses. You may wish to talk with your accountant. He or she will have suggestions for record keeping that will aid in your annual preparation.

Plan For Spending

The point of "planned" spending is not to "keep books" but to allocate expenses in advance. By planning ahead you'll control your spending and know where your money is going before it's gone, not afterward, thereby eliminating money waste.

Your checking account will serve as the basis for planned spending. What are your current spending habits? Get your checkbook with the stubs (or your cancelled checks) covering the past twelve months. On a piece of scratch paper and, using the "Planned Income Needs" (page 39) as a guide, total the past twelve months' expenses for each item. Evaluate each item. Were there any unusual expenditures? Can you reduce any? Will any increase? Pay particular attention to business-expense needs.

Evaluate your goals for the future. New automobile? Color television? Stereo? House? Vacation? College education? Then figure out what you will have to save monthly to meet these goals.

From the combined evaluation of your past spending and your future goals, you are now able to complete the "Planned Income Needs" worksheet.

How much you spend depends on you and your family. There is no strict answer, no average. The best rule is: Spend as much as you can afford for things that mean the most to you and your family. Spend as little as you can for the things that mean the least.

In your plan for spending, keep these ideas in mind:

- *Save first and spend last. This will assure that you never spend more than you earn.* If you buy something, make sure it's more than half yours.
- *If you like high living occasionally, live it up out of the money you have—not your future income.* Keep yourself liquid.
- *When you put that first little bundle in savings, leave it there.* Don't invade it. But above all, put something aside.
- *Establish a contingency reserve to draw on during periods of income fluctuations.*
- *Don't use installment credit—how can you be ahead when you're behind?* There are few things you couldn't wait six months to own. And in the end, you'll probably own more things than the individual who lacks self-control and stays in debt.

Remember, a prime advantage of your commissioned job is the opportunity to increase your income, to earn what you are worth. You control your future. Don't give yourself the "reward" before you have earned it!

It's interesting to note that the more value you place on planning, thrift, and patience, the less of a problem money management becomes.

Setting Two Kinds of Goals

As you establish your sales goals each year, you will find it very helpful to establish two kinds of goals: minimum and superior. Your minimum goals are what you must accomplish this year. There is no room for compromise with your minimum goals. *You must make a responsible commitment to them.*

Your superior goals are the things you hope to achieve—things over and above your minimum goals. *Superior goals can be considered bonus goals.*

You will want to give careful thought to your minimum goals and your superior goals. They are small keys that unlock big futures in selling. The worksheet on page 40 helps you focus on Key Production Goals and to set both minimum and superior goals.

We have always liked these words by James Russell Lowell:

Life is a leaf of paper white
whereon each one of us may write
a word or two, and then comes night.

Greatly begin! Though thou have time
but for a line, be that sublime—
not failure, but low aim, is the crime.

Lowell placed great value on aiming high. So should you!

Fixing the Action Plan

You have taken an inventory of where you are presently. You have looked at your dreams and seen where you would like to go. You have specified what you must do this year to advance toward accomplishing your goals. Now, take the process one step further, a step that will guarantee achiev-

Planned Income Needs for 19 ___

	MONTHLY	TOTAL MONTHLY	ANNUAL
FIXED EXPENSES			
Rent on mortgage payments	$ _____		
Utilities — gas, heat, light, phone, water	_____		
Disability insurance	_____		
Fire and general insurance	_____		
Property taxes	_____		
Income taxes	_____		
Social security taxes	_____		
Other	_____	$ _____	$ _____
LIVING EXPENSES			
Food	$ _____		
Clothing	_____		
Laundry and tailoring	_____		
Tobacco and non-business lunches	_____		
Auto expenses, non-business	_____		
Medical — doctor, dentist, drugs	_____		
Other	_____	$ _____	$ _____
BUSINESS EXPENSES			
Sales promotion, advertising and direct-mail, tuitions, trade assn. dues	$ _____		
Telephone, stationery, postage, supplies	_____		
Business travel and auto expense	_____		
Business entertainment	_____		
Stenographic and banking services	_____		
Other	_____	$ _____	$ _____
SAVINGS AND ACCUMULATION			
Life insurance	$ _____		
Savings account	_____		
Debt reduction (other than mortgage)	_____		
Investments	_____		
Other	_____	$ _____	$ _____
MISCELLANEOUS			
Churches and charities	$ _____		
Theater and amusements	_____		
Clubs and lodge dues	_____		
Gifts and services	_____		
Vacation	_____		
Other	_____	$ _____	$ _____
TOTAL ANNUAL REQUIREMENT			$ _____

This Year's Production Goals		
Key Production Goals	**Minimum**	**Superior**
Company Production Credits	$ _____	$ _____
MDRT Commissions	_____	_____
Paid Cases	_____	_____
Equity Sales	_____	_____
P/C Sales	_____	_____
Group Premium	_____	_____
First Year Commissions	_____	_____
Renewal Income	_____	_____
Total Income	$ _____	$ _____

Minimum goals are what you must accomplish during the year. Set them realistically high. Superior goals are optimistic, they are what you hope to achieve.

ing your expectations. Thoughtfully answer this question: *"What is it that I must do each week in order to accomplish my goals for this year?"*

You have planned your work. Now you must work your plan. When you discipline yourself to meet goals on a weekly basis, your year becomes successful. It is here — with each week's activity and results — that the victory is won.

Therefore, you must fix a weekly plan of action that will insure your success. *A weekly effort formula becomes indispensible* (see figure 2-1 on page 43). Obviously, no pat formula can be developed that will be adaptable to every agent. The activity requirement necessary for success varies according to your experience, background, and market. Then, too, this requirement changes as you gain experience, knowledge, skills, and confidence.

However, it does serve your best interest if your activity can be measured against a clearly defined standard. When you calculate your weekly effort formula, it can be a very helpful self-management tool. In Goal At-

Self-Development Goals

The selling skills I will develop this year include the following:

_____

_____

_____

The knowledge I will acquire this year (for example, LUTC, CLU, ChFC, CFP, CPCU, RHU, AMTC, company, university and industry training courses): _____

_____

_____

The habits I will strengthen include the following: _____

_____

_____

I will sharpen my selling skills and increase my average-size case to $ _____ .

My persistency will be _____ percent.

The most effective way for me to reach each of the above goals is: _____

_____

_____

_____

_____

_____

_____

_____

_____

_____

_____

_____

tainment Insurance, the weekly effort formula referred to above, you will see a guideline down the left-hand side. You can develop an individualized standard at the right-hand side that you will commit to and "live by." Building the weekly effort formula and adhering to it religiously is the equivalent of having goal-attainment insurance.

John Todd, one of the great names in life insurance history, says it's the single most important concept for you to be sold on. Belief in the weekly effort formula assures your success!

Goal-Attainment Insurance—Definitions

- *Pre-approach*—A contact call to arrange an appointment.
- *Opening Interview*—A probing, fact-finding interview to determine whether or not you have a prospect. A prospect is one who recognizes a need, has the ability to pay the premium, is insurable and is salable by you.
- *Closing Interview*—The presentation of your recommendation and the closing of the case.
- *Paid Cases*—Policy issued and case reported paid.
- *Referrals*—The name of a person who can be contacted and seen on a favorable basis. Referrals can be obtained in any of the above steps.

Making a Responsible Commitment

Nothing in the way of superior performance happens until someone makes a responsible commitment. In the contract form on page 44, you make definite the results you will achieve as a minimum for the sales year.

Plan of Action

One of the most important habits you can develop is taking time near the end of each day to plan your next day's activity. This stimulates thinking about your goals and study of how the activities you plan for the next day

This Year's Personal Performance Contract

I commit to the following objectives for this year and will do what is necessary to meet and surpass them.

Production Commitments

Paid Cases _____ MDRT Commissions $ _____

Equity Sales _____ Commissions $ _____

Property/Casualty
Group Premium $ _____

Number of New Clients _____

First-Year Persistency_____% 25-Month Persistency _____%

Financial Objectives

Earnings $ _____ Net Worth $ _____

Records to Break

Most Paid Cases in a month _____

Largest Case Sold $ _____

Most MDRT Commissions in a month $ _____

_____   _____
Date   Name

This contract form can be an important self-motivation tool if you use it properly. We suggest that you copy it or have it printed on high quality paper. Give copies to other agents in your company; it can help develop a climate for mutual goal setting. Of course, you need not share the figures you set down in your personal contract. But you do need to sign the document with the same commitment you give to any legal contract.

Figure 2-1

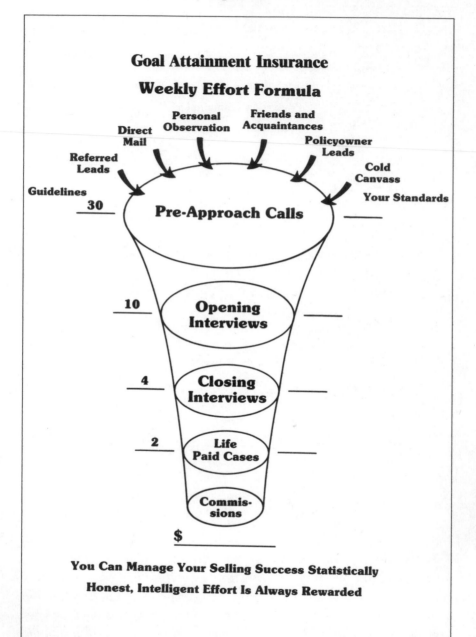

Goal Attainment Insurance

Weekly Effort Formula

Direct Mail · Personal Observation · Friends and Acquaintances · Policyowner Leads · Referred Leads · Cold Canvass

Guidelines — 30 — Your Standards

Pre-Approach Calls

— 10 — **Opening Interviews** —

— 4 — **Closing Interviews** —

— 2 — **Life Paid Cases** —

Commis-sions

$ _____

You Can Manage Your Selling Success Statistically

Honest, Intelligent Effort Is Always Rewarded

43

can help carry you forward. As W. Clement Stone points out, this planning activity helps "program" your mental computer. Your subconscious mind goes to work for you. Moreover, you *"wake up each day employed."* And that's important!

Planning comes before doing. Planning is just as important as doing. We liked what Reginald Rabjohns said in a recent MDRT presentation: "Planning encourages disciplined action—each hour spent in planning saves four hours in execution."

The planning habit doesn't come naturally. It's an "inglorious activity." It's not exciting. Planning is not going to be the highlight of your day. *However, planning your "to do" list each day is going to pay you consistent dividends.*

Activity vs Accomplishment

The type of "to do" list that you use will determine your success. One type is merely a recital of various activities, whereas *another type is a considered listing of priority items*. The first is merely a camouflage for the real thing.

To put it into perspective, consider this incident from the early 1930s, when Charles Schwab was the president of Bethlehem Steel Company. Schwab noted a productivity problem that he felt began at the top. Neither he nor his managers seemed to be accomplishing their jobs satisfactorily. He retained a well-known management consultant, Ivy Lee, to do a study. On the first day, Lee spoke briefly with Schwab and interviewed several of his top executives.

That afternoon Lee announced that he had completed his assignment. Schwab was taken aback and said he had expected the assignment to last three months. By way of explanation Lee asked Schwab to list all the activities that he personally had to accomplish in running Bethlehem Steel. "Well, that's easy enough because there are so many," Schwab said. He took about thirty minutes to list those items. Lee then requested that he revise the list, placing the tasks in the order of their importance.

This was a little more difficult and took about ninety minutes. When Schwab finished, Lee said, "My advice to you and all of your people is to accomplish each item in the order of its importance and not to go to the next until you have finished the one before."

He then closed his briefcase and asked Schwab to send him a check for whatever he felt that advice was worth. In approximately two weeks, Schwab sent Lee a check for twenty-five thousand dollars! We now say to you (for substantially less), "Go and do likewise."

Prior to establishing a "to do" list, you must determine what goals you are trying to accomplish. Arrange these goals in the order of their priority, and reflect that priority on your listing. *Otherwise, you will be mistaking activity for accomplishment.*

Many agents have taken the Plan of Action, shown on page 47, and had it produced as a pad. You may wish to do so, too. In selling, spectacular achievements can usually be traced back to unspectacular preparation.

The Mastermind

Any discussion of planning would be incomplete without a thorough examination of the mastermind principle. It's a concept that energizes your plans and can lead to their successful implementation. *The mastermind is a business alliance through which you can benefit from the experience, training, expertise, and influence of others*. It allows you to engage the minds and abilities of others as though they were really your own.

That's an amazing concept, isn't it?

A mastermind alliance is defined as two or more minds coming together in a spirit of perfect harmony for the attainment of a common objective. The interchange stimulates each individual mind to a higher performance level. An effective mastermind alliance is awesome in the enthusiasm, initiative, and creative imagination it can bring to bear on the solution of problems and employment of strategies. *When you start coordinating minds of varying background and experience in discussion of problems and opportunities, you tap sources of information not normally available to you.*

To be effective, your mastermind alliance must be active. The mere association of minds is not enough. There must be a continuous action. Each member must realize a benefit. The group must function with perfect harmony. *Remember, without the factor of harmony, the alliance may prove to be nothing more than ordinary teamwork, cooperation, or friendly co-*

46

Plan of Action

Prepare each day, at the end of your day

Name: _____ Date: _____

> Goals For This Week _____
> Yearly Objective _____
> Today's Top Priority _____

— Daily Activities —

8:00 Study Time — Self-Improvement
9:00 Self-Organization — Review today's plan, write letters, do filing, make phone calls, and handle mail. Take care of all follow-through work.

Morning Activities:
Calls and Appointments

10:00 _____
10:30 _____
11:00 _____
11:30 _____

12:00 Afternoon Activities:
Calls and Appointments

12:30 _____
1:00 _____
1:30 _____
2:00 _____
2:30 _____
3:00 _____
3:30 _____
4:00 _____
4:30 _____
5:00 _____
5:30 _____

6:00 Evening Activities:
Calls and Appointments

7:00 _____
8:00 _____
9:00 _____

> Schedule three working meals each week.

— Keeping the Score —

I. Telephone Calls to be Made
Appointments Set _____

1. _____
2. _____
3. _____
4. _____
5. _____
6. _____
7. _____
8. _____
9. _____
10. _____

II. Cases to Open _____

III. Closing Interview _____

1. _____
2. _____
3. _____
4. _____
5. _____

IV. Referrals Developed _____

1. _____
2. _____
3. _____
4. _____
5. _____
6. _____

V. Today's Results

Life and Dis. Apps. _____
Submitted MDRT $ _____
Other $ _____
Paid Cases _____
Paid MDRT $ _____
Other $ _____

ordination of effort. This is something vastly different from the master-mind principle.

The Minneapolis Mastermind

A former associate of ours, the late Dick Reed, once sold more life insurance in just nine months than he had sold in the previous twenty years. Dick had decided in March to lead our company in sales for that year. Note that he first established a *definite purpose*.

Dick quickly concluded that he couldn't accomplish his purpose by acting alone. This moved him to form his mastermind group, which he called "The Number One Club." The stated purpose of the club was to focus each year on one club member's business—and make it number one in its particular industry.

Dick Reed became the catalyst. He selected his allies carefully. He sold them on meeting each month for lunch, and he sold them on focusing on improvement of his life insurance business during the club's first year.

For each meeting, he prepared an agenda. Dick educated the group on the property of life insurance and the problems it could solve. At each meeting, he presented a report on his results so everyone was kept up-to-date on how the club was progressing toward its stated purpose. As each meeting concluded, Dick filled up an easel page with names and information about prospects referred by each of the club members.

The rest of this story is to be found in the record book. By year end, 1968, Dick Reed had sold nearly twenty-five million dollars of permanent life insurance. Not too bad, even by today's standards. The twenty-five million dollars was more life insurance than Dick Reed had sold in the previous twenty years. This was an achievement that would have been impossible without Dick's thorough application of the mastermind principle.

The Influence of a Spouse

Another practical application of the mastermind principle can be developed in the family, between an agent and a spouse. (If you don't have harmony in your home, you're usually at a great disadvantage outside in the sales world.) You'll want to get started on developing this alliance at once.

Discuss this chapter, from beginning to end, with your spouse. This chapter more than all the others will strengthen your support at home.

If you have a selling partnership with another agent, the mastermind principle is the key to its success. If you are a member of an agency, we recommend that you form an alliance with your general agent, manager, or supervisor.

The procedure that follows can truly be a fountainhead of inspiration for you. It contains a formula for generating personal power that you can use to achieve unlimited success in your insurance career.

Setting up Your Mastermind Alliance

The first step is to adopt a definite purpose as an objective to be attained by the alliance. Then choose individual members whose education, experience, and influence will make them invaluable in the achievement of that purpose.

There's no point in forming a mastermind alliance just to have someone with whom to visit. It will soon "play itself out" if you don't have a strong motive behind it. It's up to you to plant that motive in the mind of the group's members.

Your allies for this group should be chosen for their ability to help you get to where you are going. Don't choose people simply because you know them and like them or have them as friends.

You should make a careful analysis of your purpose and list the items you will need for its attainment. Then systematically go about supplying the links with which to forge the chain. Each member of the alliance should make some definite, distinctive, unique contribution to the overall picture. In addition, it should be determined what appropriate benefit each member will receive in return for his or her cooperation in the alliance.

Next, establish a definite place where the members of the alliance will meet, have a definite plan, and arrange a definite time for the mutual discussions of the plan. You will recall the importance of a plan in connection with your definite major purpose. Well, this is the time and place to reveal that plan to those harmonious associates who will have a community of interest in the success venture. You may think your plan is very good, but before you get through discussing it with your allies, you will undoubtedly modify it until you hit upon the perfect plan.

When you have established rapport between yourself and the others in your mastermind alliance, you will find that ideas will flow into the minds of each of the members, as well as your own. *Ideas will be generated that would not come to your mind alone.*

When everyone in your mastermind group meets for the round-table discussion, each member will speak with confidence and everyone will see what's on the table. There can be no secrets in such a group—if the members have been selected with care.

It's important that frequent and regular contacts be made between the members. Indefiniteness on this point, or neglect, will bring defeat. You must keep in almost continuous contact with the other minds of the group if you are to get the full benefit of them. Meetings should be scheduled often. Schedules and telephone numbers should be exchanged so that it is possible within a few minutes to discuss any sudden development with the group.

It's the burden of the leader of the alliance to see that harmony among all the members is maintained and that action is continuous in the pursuance of the definite major objective. Action or work is the connecting link between desire, plan, and fulfillment.

The watchword of the alliance should be definiteness of purpose—positiveness of plan, backed by continuous perfect harmony. The major strength of such an alliance consists in the perfect blending of the minds of all members. Jealousy, envy, or friction, as well as any lagging of interest on the part of any member, will bring defeat unless he or she is confronted immediately.

Finally, the number of individuals in an alliance should be governed entirely by the nature and magnitude of the purpose to be attained.

Most individual successes of unusual magnitude are attained through the mastermind principle, which, to define it in a slightly different way, is: A composite mind, consisting of two or more individual minds working in perfect harmony, with a definite purpose in view.

Use the mastermind principle to your advantage throughout your sales career. It will always enable you to serve others better.

Chapter Two Flashbacks

1. Selling success is the result of
   a. living one's life in _____ balance _____
   b. building a healthy _____ self image _____
   c. defining and steadfastly pursuing a series of specific, _____ realistically high goals _____
   d. setting up a _____ mastermind _____ alliance
   e. developing _____ self discipline _____ and self-management skills
   f. displaying faith and _____ perseverance _____
2. Goal setting gives clarity to your _____ chief aims _____ .
3. Ben Feldman said: "We need goals and deadlines — goals big enough to be _____ exciting _____ and deadlines to make us _____ run _____ ."
4. Goals must be _____ achievable _____ , believable, controllable, and be given _____ deadlines _____ .
5. The starting step in planning your success is _____ self assessment _____ . It's here that you examine your _____ business _____ , your personal life, and your _____ financial _____ picture.
6. As you compile your "Master Dream List," remember your only limitations are _____ self imposed _____ .
7. A yearly budget shows you the income you must produce — as a _____ minimum _____ .
8. Minimum goals are _____ committed _____ goals. Superior goals are _____ bonus _____ goals.
9. Fixing the action plan requires you to construct a _____ weekly _____ effort formula _____ .
10. Planning encourages _____ disciplined _____ action.

_____

For answers see page 230.

Self-Motivators for Improving your Planning

Review this chapter at least annually. Repeat each step in the process* every December in order to prepare yourself for the year ahead. Get into this habit and you will find that your planning will keep you on course at all times.

You already have set goals that are achievable, believable, and measurable, and you have given them deadlines, right? Following are a number of suggested self-motivators that you can use or adapt to your own planning motivation needs:

I can!
Plan your work and work your plan.
Be a good money manager.
Make no little plans.
My goal for today is _____.
Aim high!
I believe in the law of averages.
If I take care of the minutes, the years will take care of themselves.
Expect the best!

Remember as you do your daily planning for the day ahead to look for individuals who might become members of your mastermind alliance. "The mastermind principle is the medium through which we may procure the full benefit of the experience, training, education, and specialized knowledge and influence of others completely, as if their minds were in reality our own."

— Napoleon Hill

---

* The planning process developed in this chapter is available in booklet form from KIN, Inc., 17110 Dallas Parkway, Dallas, Tx. 75248.

Commentary: Get Ready, Get Set, Sell!

Your success in making a sale depends not on your prospect, but on you — on how you think, feel, and act. You can guide the prospect's thinking, feelings, and actions through suggestion. How? By conditioning your mind through self-suggestion.

A Case Study

Many years ago, as owner of Combined Registry Company, a national agency representing a large eastern insurance company selling accident-insurance protection, I personally trained my sales representatives to sell to professional and business persons and to employees in stores, offices, and banks on a cold-canvass basis. I had the exclusive rights to sell a policy known as The Little Giant.

One evening in Sioux City, Iowa, I met with one of my sales representatives who lived there. I'll never forget him. He had just returned from Sioux Center, where he had been working for two days. He was discouraged, negative, and emotional, because he hadn't made a single sale.

"I Didn't Make a Dime!"

For more than two hours, this young man griped and griped and griped. "What kind of job is this? I worked for two days away from home, paid all my expenses — my car, my meals — and I didn't make a dime!" Then he complained about Sioux Center. It was impossible to sell the people there

53

because they were Holland Dutch and clannish, he said. They would not buy from a stranger. Besides the area had suffered crop failures for the last five years.

As he talked, I changed my mind about our plans to work Sioux City the next day. This salesman needed an object lesson in how to condition his mind for selling. But I had a hard time interrupting his stream of complaints. Finally, I commanded: "STOP!"

"You have a problem," I said, then added enthusiastically, "That's terrific! With every adversity there is a seed of an equivalent or greater benefit for those who have PMA and apply it.

"Instead of working here tomorrow, just drive me to Sioux Center. I'll do the selling for most of the day, then you can sell for an hour or two. I won't interrupt you. You will prove to yourself that if you properly condition your mind, you will make sale after sale."

In a monotone, without pausing, I slowly repeated self-motivators such as, "Success is achieved by those who try and maintained by those who keep trying with PMA," and, "There is an intelligent solution to any problem if you keep your mind on what you want and off what you don't want."

He became very calm and began to listen intently. "Pray for guidance tonight," I told him. "And before you go to sleep, repeat several times to yourself, 'I will make sale after sale after sale.' Try to picture yourself making sales in the same stores you called on in the last two days."

I Conditioned my Mind

Early the next morning, the salesman picked me up in his car and we headed toward Sioux Center. As he drove along, I relaxed, closed my eyes, meditated, and conditioned my mind.

I tried to determine the reasons why I should, and would, sell these people rather than why I would not or could not—thus appealing to reason.

I said to myself, He says that they are Holland Dutch and clannish, therefore, they won't buy. That is wonderful! What is so wonderful about it? It is a well-known fact in selling that if you sell one of the clan, particularly a leader, you can sell the entire clan. All I have to do is make the first sale. This can and will be done.

The territory has had a crop failure for five years. That's an advantage for me, too. The Holland Dutch are marvelous people. They save their money. They are responsible and want to protect their families and property; yet they probably have not purchased accident insurance from other salesmen. (Years ago, relatively little accident insurance was sold to individuals; sales were to companies or through associations.) Our policies offer excellent protection at a low cost. Therefore, they are just waiting for me. I have no competition.

I Conditioned my Subconscious

I had taken the first step in mind-conditioning by appealing to reason. My problem was solved. Now it became necessary to condition my subconscious mind and my feelings.

Feelings and emotions are quickly controlled and directed by action — mental or physical. Picture the track or swimming star waiting poised a few seconds before the starting signal; that's the feeling I wanted, plus the benefits in controlling my subconscious mind and the help of a Greater Power. I wanted to get what I termed "keyed up."

While still physically relaxed with my eyes closed, I repeated to myself with sincerity, emotion, and with great rapidity for the next half hour, "Please, God, help me sell. Please, God, help me sell. Please, God, help me sell." Then I took a nap until we arrived at Sioux Center.

The First Step Toward Success

We first called at the bank, where the personnel consisted of a vice-president, a cashier, and a teller. Because of my mind-conditioning, it was impossible for the vice-president to refuse, and I knew it. Within twenty minutes, he purchased the most protection our company was willing to sell, a full unit, and he recommended that I see his son, who was the manager of the telephone company.

Then the cashier purchased. I will never forget the teller — because he didn't buy.

Beginning with the store next to the bank, I began systematically selling store after store, office after office, interviewing every individual in each establishment. We eventually got to the telephone company, where I interviewed the manager (the bank vice-president's son) and all the employees.

It was impossible to sell at Sioux Center because the people are Holland Dutch and are clannish, and because the territory has had a crop failure for five years, the salesman had said. He believed it. But I knew that every adversity has the seed of an equivalent benefit for those who have PMA and apply it. I knew that for the same reasons that it was impossible for him to sell, it would be impossible for me to fail.

We Sold Everyone in Sight

Except for the teller in the bank, I sold the full unit to every person we called on. In the afternoon, I had the salesman make calls in place after place—and he sold every person he interviewed.

While riding back to Sioux City, I thanked God for the assistance I had received, and then relaxed. The salesman returned to Sioux Center and worked for several days and experienced fantastic results. He and I had each engaged in mind-conditioning. You can, too, if you will recognize, relate, assimilate, and apply the principles in this commentary with PMA. You will . . . won't you?

I asked the question above in that particular form for a reason. Are you aware that, in selling, the technique of asking questions is one of your most important tools?

You want to become more successful in every phase of your business and personal relationships with others. Don't you? (Note: This illustrates the use of a positive statement and a question to develop a yes answer.) Of course, you do!

Ask—But Pay Attention, Too!

You may have observed that a good conversationalist asks questions about subjects of interest to the person he is talking with . . . and he pays attention to the answers. You also use questions, of course, to obtain information.

But you may not be aware of another important use of questions: to sow seeds of suggestion and direct a person's mind in a desired channel. For example, if I wanted to encourage you to help yourself and your employees by selling them on the importance of setting and achieving high goals, your mind could be directed in the desired channel by my asking: "How do you believe your life has been changed because you have set high goals?"

To formulate a response, you would have to temporarily exclude other thoughts from your mind because of the energy used in concentrating along the lines of my question. Tension would be relieved and your interest would be stimulated.

How to Use Questions

Questions that develop reflex answers are useful in the positioning technique of "breaking the ice." A simple illustration is: "How are you?" An optimist will respond, "Fine!" A pessimist will usually make some kind of complaint. I always respond, "I feel healthy . . . I feel happy . . . I feel terrific!"

If you want an affirmative response, make a positive statement and then ask an affirmative question, as I illustrated earlier. Here's another example: "You want to become more successful in every phase of your business and personal relationships with others. Don't you?" (Note that while the word *not* tends to develop a negative response, the contraction *don't*, when used in a question, aids in developing an affirmative response.)

If you want a negative response, make a negative statement and ask an affirmative question. Illustration: "You wouldn't want to miss the mark on your company goal because your employees are not aiming high enough. Would you?"

Socrates's Successful Method

Socrates had an effective system in the art of asking questions. Great salesmen frequently use his method: ask a question or a series of questions to which your prospect will readily agree, and then ask the concluding question based on those agreements. This technique allows you to force a desirable response without seeming aggressive.

—*W. Clement Stone*

Chapter Three
The Power of Positioning
Creating the Selling Climate

Whoever has a trust relationship with the individual prospect is going to get the business. This agent will come out with the sale, no matter how much information computer technology makes available.
— Kenneth Black, Jr., Ph.D.

Positioning Defined

Positioning means getting in front of decision makers and creating a selling climate that will encourage them to take action on your recommendations.

Positioning begins before the call. It starts with all the things you do to develop a favorable image in the minds of your prospects and clients. When a positive reputation precedes your contacts, your initial positioning is good.

Positioning requires a "mental readiness" that eliminates self-doubt, hesitancy, and apology from your manner and speech. We refer to this mind-set as "call courage." Displaying call courage positions you as a believable, informed, and effective agent.

Positioning means setting appointments with decision makers. This requires you to develop a confident manner when using the telephone.

Positioning depends on favorable first impressions. Generally, prospects will focus on *you* first, then on what you are selling.

Positioning depends on building relationships rather than the immediate promotion of an idea. It requires you to begin building a high level of trust right from the start.

Positioning is accomplished by probing. Probing questions uncover facts and feelings that reveal the buying motive. Your probing also helps the prospect recognize a need.

Positioning is strengthened by the promise you make to individualize the prospect's case and personalize a recommendation.

Positioning depends on understanding buyer motives. If you don't understand how and why prospects buy, your calls will always be "crapshoots," your career out of control.

Create the Right Image

Decide how you want to be perceived by prospects and clients. *You can then develop an image and a reputation that will precede you.* Reputation emerges either by choice or by chance; make sure yours is by choice and that it is the right one.

Examine the mailings you make, the business cards you carry, the advertising you do, the promptness with which you handle financial obligations, and your responsiveness in fulfilling service obligations. *Each of these, and probably others you will think of, influence to some degree the kind of perception others have of you and your business.*

We'll develop scientific ways for creating the kind of image you want to project in a later chapter on professionalism.

A Habit to Develop

At the end of a long and highly successful career, Tom Ferns, an agent in Akron, Ohio, was asked for the most important advice he could give young agents. He responded: "Tell them to start early and stay late. Most of all, remind them how important it is to learn to pay attention." Paying attention is a habit you can develop. It will keep your mind on the data that your eye and ear bring it — considering, forming opinions, planning, estimating, weighing, balancing, and calculating.

Paying attention is a key to consistently increasing your production. It provides you with clues on how you can best build the all-important selling relationship. When you move to the interview, paying attention helps you pinpoint needs. As you move to the close, it helps you recognize buying signals.

Paying attention pays!

Napoleon Hill made "controlled attention" one of his seventeen Principles of Success. He said, "This is the principle through which the mind may be focused upon one objective, to the exclusion of all others, until that one objective is attained. Controlled attention is the highest form of self-discipline." W. Clement Stone says, "The value and benefit of your creative-thinking time depends to a large extent on your ability to control your attention and focus your thoughts on your goals." As you will see, paying attention is also critical to the important business of prospecting.

Build Your Reservoir

The basic ingredient of positioning is people you can see under favorable conditions. Prospecting — building a reservoir of such people as prospective clients — is an important part of staying positioned.

If you are to achieve superior selling results, prospecting must become as natural to you as breathing. It will, if you conscientiously and consistently do these two things:

1. *Pay Attention* — As Tom Ferns indicated, a successful agent is observant. Keep your eyes and ears open. Do more than just look; see something. Do more than listen; hear something. Make notes. Develop an alertness and a probing, inquisitive attitude. Paying attention alerts you to new prospects and the best reasons and ways to contact them. Paying attention prompts you to learn as much as possible about prospects before you make the initial contact.

Ben Feldman advises us to "Listen with three ears. Ear number one permits you to hear what your prospects say. Listening with ear number two, you hear what they don't say. And with the third ear, you hear what your prospects wanted but didn't know how to say." Paying attention can become one of the greatest factors in your selling career. Paying attention is a powerful mental process. Form this habit now and practice it from now on.

2. *Maintain an Action File*—Here's where you place prospect cards and other important follow-up information. The primary purpose of such a file is to provide you with a system for bringing names of prospective clients to your attention at a time when it's best to make contact with them.

Don't develop a hope chest. It's not a sign of success to have a bulging file of "dead wood." A box of names can invite you to spend idle hours sorting and resorting cards. *Determine as early as possible whether or not the person is a prospect for you.* The only "reservoir-building" file that works is one that contains bona fide prospects—individuals who will appreciate the kind of work you do and the products you sell. It's better to develop a reservoir of five hundred legitimate prospects than to have a collection of several thousand suspects! *The good prospector with a well-organized, active "reservoir-building" file will have to work hard to find enough time to contact and work with all of the prospective clients he or she has.*

You live and sell today in a generation of hustle-bustle. Taking time-out for thinking and organization is sometimes considered "idling your motor." At one time, prospecting itself may have been thought of as taking time-out from selling. But today, successful agents place prospecting near the top on their list of priorities when they think about positioning.

The value of a well-organized prospect file cannot be overrated. *Professionals regard their file of prospective clients in the same light as their personal bank account.*

Let's examine the major methods of building a reservoir of qualified prospects.

- *Personal Observation*—The single best source of prospects are those you develop through personal observation and personal contacts. Think in terms of people everywhere you go. Your present sphere of influence can literally be a gold mine. *Develop an awareness of people who are in transition periods in their lives.* Prospects facing a new situation often realize that it will affect their financial position. Frequently, this will provide an impetus for action.

Once you become prospect-minded, you'll develop "a nose for business" as keen as a reporter's "nose for news." It's another way of saying that you formed the habit of paying attention.

- *Centers of Influence* — The center-of-influence strategy develops a number of key people who serve as "centers" that feed information and prospects to you. These are individuals who want to be helpful and who want you to do well. In some cases, these "centers" will be clients. In other instances, they will be relatives and influential friends who are willing and able to cooperate.

Centers of influence should be a consistent, reliable source of quality prospects. For example, your spouse can feed you good names each week. Friends, select clients, and influential contacts will provide you names on a regular basis when cultivated properly. *Employing this strategy successfully puts your credibility on the line.* No one is going to give a lot of thought to helping you unless they know you are a deserving, competent professional.

- *Client Referrals* — Most new clients will provide you with referral information and introductions if they are asked properly. The reason is that people enjoy being influential in the success of a friend or an associate. Your attitude should always be, "Whom can I now contact on a favorable basis because I developed this client?"

Always strive to get introductions and information from your new clients. Practice this skill in developing referrals. *Remember, getting one introduction to a referral you will approach and develop as a client is much better than a list of names that don't spark your enthusiasm to make the initial call.* After you have been in the business a few years, you should find your clients becoming your strongest source of new business. Naturally, clients continue to buy from you as they progress and their needs change. We will develop several referred-lead strategies for you in chapter five.

- *Direct-Mail Lists* — You can purchase lists of names, addresses, and telephone numbers broken down by demographic characteristics. Look in the Yellow Pages to find mailing-list brokers. You can buy preaddressed labels with the names and addresses of almost any category of prospects.

Dun & Bradstreet can help you identify business owners and key executives. They will provide you with a wealth of information about local businesses.

The best agents tend to find "nests" of people in which to work. These are groups of people who have a common interest. Working in nests is generally more profitable than seeking out and finding prospects who have no connection with one another. It makes it possible for you to become known as the expert in the problems and the needs of the group. Because the group is usually located in a single geographic area, you can cover more ground and become better known in less time. Developing nests makes for direct-mailing efficiency.

Make Friends to Make Sales

The sure way to improve your odds in selling is to cultivate the art of getting people to like you. Prospects buy from the agent they want to buy from, and they make premium and all other decision factors fit.

President Lyndon Johnson kept on his desk this list of "Ten rules for getting people to like you":

1. Remember names and use them.
2. Be a comfortable person to deal with so there is no strain in doing business with you. Be an "old-shoe, an old-hat" kind of individual.
3. Acquire the quality of not being easily ruffled.
4. Guard against giving the impression that you know it all, even in those instances where you do.

5. Cultivate the quality of being an idea person, so others will get something of value from their association with you.
6. Study to get the "scratchy" elements out of your personality.
7. Drain off your grievances. Attempt to heal misunderstandings.
8. Practice liking people until it becomes second nature.
9. Never miss the opportunity to pay a compliment.
10. Offer encouragement — it's the oxygen of the soul.

Agents who stay at the top specialize in making friends. It makes sales and establishes clients. Lots of them!

Expect the Best

Everything about you — your facial expression, your eye contact, your movements, your dress, the tone of your voice, your handshake, your posture — tells your prospects what you think of yourself.

There is no known law by which you can achieve selling success without first expecting it. Superior selling results are produced by the perpetual expectation of attaining them. Despite natural talents and thorough training and education, selling achievements seldom rise higher than the expectation. "They can who think they can — they can't who think they can't," is an inflexible, indisputable law of selling and, actually, of life itself.

As a professional agent, your self-confidence is the one thing you can *never* afford to surrender. Count as an enemy the person who shakes your estimate of your selling ability. Nothing enhances your ability as an agent more than faith in yourself. In our business, faith can turn a one-talent agent into a multimillion-dollar producer; but without it, a ten-talent individual remains mediocre.

The agent who is self-reliant, positive, optimistic, and assured charges the atmosphere around him with electricity. This kind of agent has an aura of command that helps convince prospects that he or she can deliver. Set your mind so resolutely, so definitely, and with such determined expectations toward the cases and MDRT credits you desire, that nothing will sway your purpose.

Develop Call Courage

The World Insurance Group of a major financial institution sponsored a survey of Million-Dollar-Round-Table members. The members were asked to rate a series of personal attributes relative to succeeding in selling. The attribute ranked "most important" in this survey was *self-confidence*. There are a lot of reasons for call reluctance, and all of them get in the way of successful selling. Learning how to arm yourself against the self-defeating effect of negative encounters is a "must lesson" for anyone aiming for success as an agent.

Whether or not you are conscious of it, you carry into every selling situation a rather definite picture of yourself. The stronger your purpose and the belief in what you are selling, the more likely you are to project yourself as an intelligent, informed, competent agent.

Right from the start, you want to eliminate timidness, hesitancy, and apology from both your manner and speech. Here's something from Shakespeare that has helped us a lot over the years: "Our doubts are traitors, and make us lose the good we oft might win by fearing to attempt." Joe Epkins, a perennial MDRT performer in Chicago, says: "The obstacle every agent must hurdle to achieve greater results is call reluctance. As agents, we are tempted to dodge the chance of a turndown because it does damage to our self-image."

You'll learn to cope with call reluctance and to build call courage by following these five suggestions:

1. *Stay sold on what you are selling.*
2. *Saturate your mind with positive, upbeat feelings.* Tell yourself that you're enthusiastic and effective. You're prepared and persuasive. Take these "mental vitamins" regularly and you'll keep yourself up to trigger favorable responses.
3. *Prepare yourself technically.* Know your product; learn your lines; prepare so that your presentations are as natural as your breathing. Knowing all about your ideas and learning your lines gives you a competitive edge. It builds your persuasion power — your call courage.
4. *Focus on the rewards of success.* Don't think about the penalties of failure. Remember, your next call can result in a sale that can

change your entire week or month. Imagine how you'll feel after this kind of experience. You can control what you imagine. Feelings follow thought. Act the way you want to feel.

5. *Remind yourself that most people are nice people.* Remember, prospects often fail to show they are nice during the early minutes of an initial contact. Prospects are often tense and nervous and act a bit "abnormal"—as though they aren't too nice. This is an even stronger reason for you to stay in control and act like a poised, confident professional. *Let prospects key off of your attitude—never key off of theirs.*

Call courage must be developed if you are to succeed as an agent. You must conquer call reluctance. As the late Dr. Maxwell Maltz, the distinguished plastic surgeon and author of *Psycho-Cybernetics*, always said: "The surest way to develop courage is to act courageous. Do the thing you fear—and do it now! Call courage will follow."

Take the Pledge

Before we examine a new psychology of selling, memorize the following pledge. Feed it into your mental computer and keep it on instant recall for the rest of your selling career.

I will never begin talking to a prospect on the telephone, in a seminar, or on an interview until I have written out my script, rehearsed and learned the lines so they can be expressed naturally, conversationally, and persuasively.

Taking this pledge will assure your effectiveness for these reasons: First, you say the right thing, consistently, not occasionally. Second, you tell your story in the fewest words. Third, it gives you more confidence because you know what you're going to say.

Many successful agents owe their substantial production and earnings today to "taking the pledge."

The New Psychology of Selling

The traditional way to sell insurance was to approach prospects, advise them, appeal to them, persuade them, and make the sale. Such a selling

Figure 3-1

EAT YOUR WAY
TO THE TOP

Gene Foxen, an agent for New England General, says: "If you're skipping breakfast and brown-bagging lunch at your desk, you're missing out on some of the selling time available.

"Some successful agents have as many as three breakfast appointments ('Just coffee, thanks. I'm on a diet.') and at least one luncheon appointment every day.

"The advantages are obvious. First, the best, most relaxed conversations tend to take place while people are breaking bread together. It's natural. You have a chance to relax, eat, and talk. It's not a tense business meeting, but something of a social occasion. This makes prospects more receptive.

"Second, a working breakfast or lunch doesn't cut into your business time. Since everybody has to eat, it can ease the 'no time' objection when setting up an appointment.

"A third advantage of working this way is that it increases your daytime activity."

style often resulted in sales pressure that produced a combative, defensive state of mind in the prospect. Frequently, it didn't get the sale made. If a sale was made, in many instances it didn't lead to a satisfied client.

Our experience in recent years provides evidence that casts considerable doubt on the wisdom of the "traditional selling style." The procedure that appears to be far more effective in influencing today's sophisticated buyers is: *encourage them to communicate with you*. Get them to express their feelings and ideas. Help them verbalize their needs and genuinely participate with you in the "selling" process.

A sale, by our definition, is: *a decision in favor of the action you are proposing*. The prospect first decides to grant you an interview under favorable conditions. He or she then participates further by agreeing to give you full and complete information, to provide you medical history or have a medical checkup, and to let you pick up his or her policies. Finally, the prospect agrees to act on your recommendation for additional insurance and makes the necessary premium outlay.

The sales process we advocate causes your prospect to participate and to make a series of decisions in favor of the action you are proposing. Thus, he or she feels friendlier toward you and develops more feeling of participation as the selling process continues. Your prospect feels motivated from within rather than compelled by an outside, opposing force.

The procedure we recommend generally leads to a multiple-interview sale. Note, however, that in certain situations a package sale can and should be made on a one-interview basis. In the case of home-service agents, where there is continual contact with the prospect, one-interview selling is many times advisable and can be done effectively. In most instances, however, it would be illogical to attempt to "cover all the ground" in fewer than two interviews.

The Client-Building Process

The building of a satisfied client requires an understanding of six clearly defined, totally independent sales. In other words, the sales process consists of a *series* of sales. You make each of these sales in a step-by-step sequence:

Sale no. 1 — Setting an appointment
Sale no. 2 — Developing need recognition
Sale no. 3 — Gaining agreement to take a serious look
Sale no. 4 — Securing the app and check
Sale no. 5 — Establishing a client
Sale no. 6 — Getting referred lead endorsements

This client-building process is shown graphically in figure 3-2, on page 71. It begins with the prospecting reservoir and moves around the track, through each of the six sales. The sixth sale generates referred-lead introductions, which replenish your prospecting reservoir, and the process begins again.

The first sale is generally handled by telephone. The second and third sales will normally be made on your initial interview. Usually, qualifying the prospect properly takes all the time allotted to a first interview. You do not want to be limited by time when you move to the presentation of your recommendation, so it's best to split the first interview into two distinct parts, each of which has a specific purpose. You then handle the fourth sale on a second interview. Of course, in certain situations the second, third, and fourth sales can be handled effectively on the initial interview. Making these sales on a single interview generally revolves around simple package plans, (i.e., mortgage cancellation, pension maximization, educational funding). Whether you move with a single-interview or multiple-interview strategy, the fifth and sixth sales are made when you deliver the contract to the insured.

Use of a two-interview strategy, when learned well during the early months of your career, will pave the way for you to successfully and professionally complete the series of sales that comprise the purchase of insurance. Later, when you are ready to move into the sophisticated, advanced underwriting markets, you will find the two-interview system to be a necessity.

Route Map For Building Clients

Laid out schematically, the process of building clients resembles a racetrack (and it is!). It is an endless loop consisting of six zones, each of which comprises a separate sale.

Figure 3-2

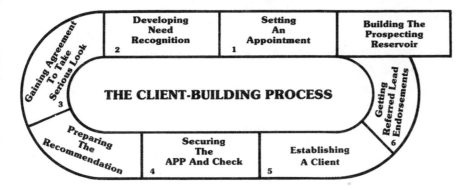

Developing Need Recognition 2	Setting An Appointment 1	Building The Prospecting Reservoir

Gaining Agreement To Take Serious Look 3

THE CLIENT-BUILDING PROCESS

Getting Referred Lead Endorsements

Preparing The Recommendation

| Securing The APP And Check 4 | Establishing A Client 5 | 6 |

Explanation of the Client-Building Process

	Building the Prospecting Reservoir	Organize the names of people in locations in which you have a definite reason for making a contact.
Sale no. 1	Setting an Appointment	Make contact to establish the time and location for the initial interview.
Sale no. 2	Developing Need Recognition	Probe to uncover facts and feelings. Decide upon the need, buying motive, and who decision maker is.
Sale no. 3	Gaining Agreement to Take a Serious Look	Explain your service. Develop a premium commitment, pick up information and policies. Arrange your next interview.
	Preparing the Recommendation	Send follow-up letter to prospect. Study and analyze information. Develop personalized recommendation. Plan and confirm next interview.
Sale no. 4	Securing the App and Check	Review the previous interview. Present the recommendation and close the business.
Sale no. 5	Establishing a Client	Make the sale solid.
Sale no. 6	Getting Referred Lead Endorsements	Make the sale productive.

Making Sale No. 1

Setting an Appointment is almost always done by telephone. This is a key sale and one you must learn to make confidently. *Knowing what you are going to say and how you are going to say it is a definite confidence builder*. Here's an example of the kind of script we recommend you adopt for making this sale by telephone:

Hello, Pete. (Response) *This is Rick McLaughlin calling. Bill Bates asked me to call, Pete, and I promised him I would. Is this a convenient time for you to talk?* (Response)

Pete, I'm in the insurance business with Mass Mutual here in Dallas. (Don't pause) *Now, I'm not calling because I have any reason to believe you're in the market for insurance. However, we know that when you purchased life insurance in the past, you probably purchased from a reliable company and from someone you knew. And as you progress and make additional purchases, the chances are, you will buy on the same basis.*

Pete, sometime soon I'd like the opportunity to talk with you and tell you about an unusual service we have designed to help our clients better plan and organize their life insurance and financial programs. In your line of business, Pete, when would be the best time for us to get together? Are mornings or afternoons better for you?

How to Chase Early Resistance

You will encounter resistance on your initial contact. Anticipate it. Don't get detoured by it.

The amount and nature of the resistance depends upon the strength of the relationship you and/or your referral have with the prospect.

Your strategy for dealing with the early resistance should go like this:

(1) Ignore the resistance and again ask for the appointment.
(2) If your prospect still resists, ask a question. *When is the last time you had your insurance reviewed?*
(3) If you still get resistance, you will want to use this resistance-chasing strategy: *I would appreciate very much your courtesy in giving me thirty minutes—just thirty minutes—to show you the kind of work we are doing for our many clients today. In your line of business, (name), are mornings or afternoons better for you?*

Develop Tele-Confidence

The telephone is the one business tool that helps budget time, develop interest, and enhance your image as a professional. By making use of the telephone, you

- *increase your number of contacts and reduce the cost per contact.*
- *improve your effectiveness.* It is often possible to gain the ear of a busy prospect when you can't gain a face-to-face interview.
- *encourage brevity.* Concentration is required on both ends of the wire.
- *have an opportunity to obtain an immediate decision.*

Some basic "How-to" telephone strategies you'll want to employ are shown in exhibit 3-1. However, there are four key strategies on which your success with the telephone depends. These are:

1. *Have a reason for calling.* Have something to discuss that motivates the person at the other end to want to listen.
2. *Be prepared to respond.* Be mentally and physically "ready to strike."
3. *Follow a prepared script.* Know what you are going to say and how you are going to say it. Your first ten words are critical to your success.

73

4. *Be brief and convey a certain sense of urgency by speaking a bit faster and louder than normal.*

Developing competence and confidence in using the telephone can boost your sales performance dramatically.

Using a Pre-Approach Letter

In making Sale no. 1, a growing trend among successful agents and financial planners is the use of a preapproach letter. Sometimes it's better to send out preapproach letters before contacting prospects by phone. You will want to follow up on each letter with a personal contact within three to five days. Figure 3-3 shows a letter that is working well for Curt Ladd, an MDRT agent in Dallas. This letter can be adapted to nearly any situation. Generally, it's mailed to someone Curt knows or to a prospect who will know him. You can easily revise the letter to fit referrals. You can even use it for mass mailing to relatively "cold" prospects. It's the kind of letter that can be written on your behalf by a satisfied client.

Telemarketing

Several high-producing agents believe telemarketing to be an idea whose time has come. David Jones, a newcomer and already a company leader for Prudential in Naples, Florida, talks about his success with telemarketing. David says, "I entered the life insurance business in April of 1985 with an already heavy budget requirement. It was necessary for me to move to a fast, productive start. In telemarketing, I found the answer to my main question: How am I going to best utilize my time (and money) and be as productive as possible? [The payoff of David's telemarketing approach was that at age twenty-six—in his first calendar year of selling—he produced an incredible thirteen million dollars!]

"All of us know we are at our best when we are in front of prospects," David adds. "The telemarketing strategy I use keeps me in front of qualified prospects. I hire older women to call three hours a day to develop qualified leads. The ladies use a simple, relaxed preapproach that goes like this:

"'May I speak to Floyd Smith? Mr. Smith, this is Ann Reynolds calling from Prudential. We have some tax-deferred programs that, with the new Tax Reform Act, have become very popular. *We would like to give you a proposal with no obligation.* Could you provide me your birth date? And your wife's? Please expect a call from David Jones, who will develop the proposal and deliver it to you in the next few days. Thank you.' Our prospects seem to be receptive to this type of contact because they are not committing to anything. We have aroused their curiosity.

"When I call a few days later, I introduce myself and remind Floyd that my secretary talked to him the other day about some of Prudential's tax-favored plans. 'She gave me your birth date of 1-1-26 and your wife's of 3-7-30, is that correct?' I then let them know that I have already prepared the proposal she promised and would like to take about twenty minutes or so to deliver it to him.

"Our solicitors generate three to four leads an hour. The objectives of their call is to generate curiosity and get enough personalized information so that I have a reason for making an appointment. Unlike x-dating, the prospects can't get an explanation or quote over the phone. Having birth dates lets me know what to propose, whether it be annuities, single-pay life, or mutual funds.

"I have found this system to be extremely successful in the over-fifty-five market. Here the prospects generally have time during the day for a visitor. They also usually have money and are interested in tax-saving ideas.

"The telephone has proven to be the quickest and most cost-effective way for me to get in front of a large number of qualified prospects. More importantly, I don't have to deal with all the resistance and rejection that always go with cold-calling selling."

Exhibit 3-1—"How-To" Telephone Pointers

1. *Maintain a positive mental attitude about using the telephone.* Always have a specific reason for calling. Always be mentally and physically "ready to strike." Know the "dollar value" of each telephone call you make. Stay sold on the law of averages.
2. *Build and use a script.* Know exactly what you are going to say and how you are going to say it. Your first ten words are critical to your

success. Use statements—not questions. Make certain there is no apology in what you say or how you say it.

3. *Smile before you dial.* Be brief and convey a sense of urgency in your voice by speaking a bit faster.

4. *Use the magical words and expressions to assure a favorable first impression.* "(Name of person who gave referral) asked me to call and I promised him I would. Is this a convenient time for you to talk?" Verify the name of the prospect to whom you are speaking, if you have any question. Make certain of its pronunciation.

5. *Choose a private place to make your calls*—you need to establish momentum and avoid interruptions.

6. *Organize your calls.* Have names, numbers, and thoughts organized in advance. You will accomplish more in less time when you do. Your prospects and clients will be impressed by your organization. Call referred leads, client mail replies, etc., first—and as soon as you receive them.

7. *Seek some common ground with the person at the other end of the line.* Do you have mutual acquaintances? Do you know about his or her work, neighborhood, community involvement?

8. *Speak as if you were with the prospect and looking directly at him or her.* This helps to establish rapport. Courtesy, sincerity, and clarity of speech are essential to your success. Use "Thank you," "May I ask," and other expressions that demonstrate good manners. Keep a smile in your voice.

9. *Be assertive.* Assertiveness shows itself in your voice quality. When you speak on the telephone, your voice is you and your business. The impression it makes has a big influence on your prospect's decisions as to whether or not to give you an appointment. Be and stay enthusiastic; it will come through in your voice.

10. *Avoid an argument.* No matter what the prospect's response is, stay poised and point toward the setting of an appointment. Use questions that invite "yes" answers. Don't push too hard for an appointment and never accept an appointment that sounds tentative. Make sure the prospect understands that your time is valuable.

Figure 3-3

FIRST
FINANCIAL
CENTER

CURT LADD
President

Mr. Oscar Ponder, President
Ponder Products, Inc.
6090 Campbell Road, Suite 122
Dallas, Texas 75248

Dear Oscar:

We have been successful in our efforts to develop and provide a complete life-insurance service for clients who are in situations similar to yours. We believe our service will be of interest to you.

I am not writing because we have any reason to believe that you are about to buy life insurance. On the other hand, we know that when you bought life insurance in the past, you probably bought from a reliable company and from someone you knew. In the future, when you make additional purchases, chances are you will buy in the same manner.

Depending upon the circumstances, I plan to call for an appointment or stop at your office in the next week. Please be assured, Oscar, that this call will not be turned into a selling interview for life insurance. You might say it will be an attempt to "sell myself" and to explain our unique service.

Thanks in advance for what I hope will be your approval of my call.

Yours sincerely,

Curtis T. Ladd

CTL/laf

Make a Favorable Impression

As you move to the initial face-to-face contact, *always look and dress like someone your prospects would go to for financial advice.* The first things prospects notice are your general appearance, your facial expression, your voice, and your teeth. Appearance is often all prospects have to judge you on until your full message is delivered. You owe it to yourself to consistently make favorable impressions. You never know who may be influenced favorably by one of those impressions.

Here's an interesting example of what can happen:

An elderly lady stepped into an interior decorator's shop to get out of the rain. All the clerks ignored her—except one young man, who asked if he might help.

"No," she said, "I'm just looking around, waiting for the rain to let up a bit."

Instead of walking away, as many clerks would have done, he stayed and talked to her. When she was ready to leave, he gave her his card, escorted her to the street, and assisted her in finding a cab.

A week later, the lady phoned and gave the clerk an order amounting to several thousand dollars. Mrs. Andrew Carnegie had been so impressed by the young man's courtesy that she wanted him to go to Scotland to help her furnish her Skibo Castle!

A rare coincidence? A thing like that couldn't happen to you? Don't be too sure. The impression you make with each telephone call and contact call can, and does, make a difference. First impressions do last.

As Chicago psychologist Dr. Irwin Ross said: "Fortunately, making a good first impression is not a matter of mysterious magnetism or of 'getting a break.' It's a skill that anyone can acquire." Anyone, that is, who stays aware of the importance of developing the skill.

Actually, you have two chances to make a good first impression—and both are on your initial calls with prospects. The first is by telephone; the second is when you make the initial face-to-face contact. During these contacts your prospects are sizing you up, deciding if you're a prepared, interesting, qualified professional.

It's important to have a plan of action for every call and interview, but it's especially critical on the very first contact. You're seeking acceptance, building confidence, and laying the foundation for a productive relationship.

Use the Impression Builders

Here are some practical ways in which you can make favorable first impressions:

- Be punctual.
- Believe you are really worth meeting, knowing, and listening to, and you will be.
- Display a clean and businesslike appearance.
- Project a pleasant disposition.
- Remember names and use them.
- Have a confident, enthusiastic manner.
- Never miss the opportunity to pay a compliment.
- Be well-mannered and courteous.
- Develop an insight into your prospect's known and probable needs.
- Be a comfortable person to deal with so there is no strain in doing business with you.

Future sales interviews will generate results in direct proportion to your all-important first contact call. Make it count.

Remember, there's no second chance to make a good first impression.

Build Trust

Trust is a feeling. It's fragile. It takes time and effort to build trust, but only an instant to destroy it.

The most fundamental approach to building relationships of trust is to recognize that most prospects have one thing in common: *the need to be appreciated and to feel important.*

Provide for your prospects what Dr. David Schwartz of Georgia State refers to as "ego food." He says "ego food" comes in these "five brands":

- Compliment the prospect's appearance
- Congratulate achievements

- Recognize family members, who they are, or what they have done
- Make the prospect look smart
- Acknowledge possessions in which the prospect takes pride.

We add to the above two "ego-food supplements" of our own:

- Ask for the prospect's advice and opinion
- Use the prospect's name regularly and be certain of its pronunciation.

"Ego food" can be a powerful substance and effective as a relationship-builder, providing, of course, that it's believable. *Be authentic with all of your expressions*. This builds belief, credibility, and trust.

Two other trust-building strategies you'll want to employ are consistency and information sharing. Prospects tend to trust agents who are consistent and predictable in their behavior. Such things are punctuality, returning telephone calls, and making good on promises are some of the ways in which you will be measured.

Referring business to prospects or clients or sharing information that will help them in their work in some way is another surefire means of building relationships.

Relationships make the world go 'round. Your prospects are human and social as well as interested in insurance and investments. You must appeal to both sides. Your prospects may claim to be motivated by intellect alone, but the professional agent knows that they run on both logic and emotions.

Become skillful at building relationships of trust. It positions you for bigger and better sales—and more of them.

Developing Need Recognition

The primary objective of the first interview is to determine whether this person has the qualities necessary to make him or her a prospect for you. You are there to qualify or disqualify. This is Sale no. 2, Developing Need Recognition. When you determine that you have a qualified prospect, you then gather full and complete information with the promise that it will be studied carefully and a recommendation (proposal) will be prepared for his or her consideration.

This opening interview must arouse the prospect's interest and turn needs into wants. If conducted properly, it will also give you important information, data that allows you to answer several qualifying questions: Is there recognition of a need? Are there dollars available for premiums? Is the person insurable? Can you make the sale?

Selling assists the prospect in making certain decisions in your favor, one decision at a time. A most important decision has already been made—the decision to grant you an appointment.

The label we give to the first stage of your probing process is *the approach*. Presumably, it's the first actual meeting between you and your prospect. The approach has two objectives: (1) to make a favorable impression upon your prospect, and (2) to arouse positive interest in listening to you.

During the approach, build an atmosphere of trust so that the prospect will have an open mind to your ideas and suggestions. Condition the prospect to consider your recommendations logically.

To develop the recognition of a need with your prospect, you'll want to ask such probing questions as:

May I ask, (name), in addition to your group insurance and any term insurance you have, with what companies do you own your personal, permanent life insurance?

Are you familiar with the new interest-sensitive insurance plans that give you the opportunity to accumulate substantial funds with tax-sheltered interest accumulations?

What do you want done with the mortgage on your home if something should happen to you?

What type of education do you plan for your children? Have you checked the cost of providing a college education? What provisions are you making for accumulating educational funds?

Have you ever considered what percentage of your present standard of living you would like to have your family maintain if you don't live to see them through?

May I ask, (name), have you made provisions through your life-insurance program to maximize your pension income at retirement? It's important to plan for the possibility of premature death, but it's also important to plan for the very real probability that you are going to live.

If you should become sick or hurt and can't work, (name), how much monthly income would you need to maintain your current standard of living? How long would your savings last if your earned income stopped today?

In your opinion, if you feel your new, interest-sensitive plan is the best and most complete you've seen, how much can you set aside each month?

The best way to get your prospect to think and recognize a need is to ask questions—relevant questions. In many cases, it's the *only* way you can get the prospect to think.

Prospects seldom buy anything unless they feel it's in their interest and benefit to do so. One of the surest ways to increase your selling effectiveness is to learn more about what your prospects want. Strategic, probing questions develop this kind of information.

Uncover Feelings

Creative selling depends upon uncovering prospect's feelings about certain needs. You may find it helpful to involve your prospects in completing a "feeling-finding" exercise like the one shown in exhibit 3-2.

Improve Probing

We agree with Roger Zener, the well-known Portland consultant, when he says: "If you want to improve an agent's effectiveness and production, improve the probing questions he or she asks of prospects." As Roger says: "When in doubt, ask a question." Exhibit 3-3 provides you ten probing investment questions. In exhibit 3-4 Equitable's Prudence Harker of Beloit, Wisconsin, shares with us the strategic questions she uses effectively in business interviews.

Remind yourself to pay attention and constantly look for the prospect's "hot button." For most people there is some problem area of their lives in

Exhibit 3-2 — How Do You Feel?

Please check the box that most closely describes your feelings about each statement.

    (A) Essential   (B) Important   (C) Unimportant

	(A)	(B)	(C)
1. Professional assistance in planning my insurance and financial matters is	☐	☐	☐
2. Owning adequate life insurance on my life is	☐	☐	☐
3. My spouse believes an adequate insurance program is	☐	☐	☐
4. Arranging to maintain my family at their standard of living after my death is	☐	☐	☐
5. Paying off the mortgage on my home in the event of my death is	☐	☐	☐
6. Planning retirement income is	☐	☐	☐
7. Having income to replace my earnings if I become sick or am injured is	☐	☐	☐
8. Financial planning, including estate planning and tax considerations, is	☐	☐	☐
9. Wills and will planning are	☐	☐	☐
10. A good understanding of my needs, objectives, and priorities by my insurance counselor is	☐	☐	☐

which life insurance, an equity product, or disability income is the best solution. It might be mortgage insurance, educational insurance, disability income, life insurance, or retirement income. It could be business insurance or any one of a number of other priorities. But the only way you have of discovering the prospect's "hot button" is through a planned, fact-and-feeling-finding procedure. Using such an approach, you will gather both tangible and intangible information. You'll have a definite idea of the prospect's attitude toward insurance and equities, his or her family, and you. As Ben Silver says: "Most selling is done by listening."

The Power of Probing — An Illustration

Harold Zlotnik has been a Round-Table member for twenty-six years. He is a member of the Top of the Table. Harold believes in the strategic questioning approach to arousing the prospect's interest, and he shares this effective, five-minute, interest-arouser. This is a probing idea you may find to be quite effective.

Bill is an architect, about thirty-five years old. He and I have been sitting over a cup of coffee for a few minutes, and I say something like this to him:

"Bill, do you have a will?"

He says, "Yes."

I say, "Well, tell me what it says."

Bill says, "Well, I leave everything to my wife."

And if he doesn't have a will, I have learned something, haven't I? And then I will probably say something like this: "Well, Bill, if you had a will what would it say? In any case he answers, "I'd leave everything to my wife."

And I say, "What's everything?"

Bill says, "Well, I have the house, the car, a few investments, and some life insurance."

And I say, "Well, if you had died last night, what would she do with all that?"

And Bill says, "What do you mean?"

I say, "Does she get an income, or does she start cashing assets, just how does she handle the whole thing?"

Bill says, "Of course I want her to have an income."

And I ask, "How much income?"

Bill says, "Well, let's see, about twenty to thirty thousand dollars a year."

I say, "Is that to spend, or does she have to pay taxes on that?"

Bill says, "Well, at thirty thousand dollars she'd have some taxes to pay. I think I'd like her to have thirty thousand."

And I say, "Bill, if I'd asked you that question five years ago, what would the answer have been?"

Bill says, "Well, about five years ago, the answer would have been about half, about fifteen thousand dollars."

I say, "Bill do you think inflation is going to continue?"

Bill says, "Of course."

And then I'll probably ask the most important question of all. "Bill, how important is it to you that your wife gets that thirty thousand dollars per year? How important is it?" I get almost the same answer word for word every time.

Bill says, "Real important!" He loves his wife.

I say, "O.K., how much capital would you have to have to produce thirty thousand of income?"

Bill says, "Well, if I understand your question, at say ten percent interest, I would think you need a little over three hundred thousand dollars."

Now, I haven't given Bill any answers, I am asking questions. He is educating me and educating himself. Bill is doing the thinking. His receiver is on, he's transmitting and he can feel the problem.

I now say, "That sounds about right—are you expecting to inherit any money?"

Bill says, "No."

I say, "How much capital do you have now, that can be used to produce income?"

Bill says, "Well, let's see. I have seventy-five thousand dollars of insurance, twenty-five thousand in my company pension plan, and I have another twenty-five thousand in investments, cash, etc. That total is about one hundred twenty-five thousand dollars.

I say, "Well, let us see now, how much are you short?"

He starts to figure. Oops . . . this is the moment of discovery, isn't it? He says, "Let's see, three hundred thousand minus one hundred twenty-five thousand, that's one hundred seventy-five thousand dollars—I need one hundred seventy-five thousand dollars."

And I say, "Where are you going to get one hundred seventy-five thousand dollars in a hurry, Bill?"

Bill says, "You son of a gun! How much would life insurance cost?"

Now I haven't made any statement, I haven't proposed anything, I've just asked questions. I haven't judged any of his answers. It has taken about five minutes for this very simple interview and it gets the prospect thinking and interested.

Exhibit 3-3–Proven, Probing Investment Questions

1. What has been your must successful investment? How much have you invested and kept invested in the last five years?

2. How do you reduce your taxes?

3. What are you doing to maximize return on your bank savings or money-market accounts?

4. What are you doing to generate meaningful capital gains?

5. What are you doing to provide for your retirement?

6. What services of your investment consultant have you found the most useful?

7. What investments are you concerned about?

8. How could your investment consultant improve his or her service?

9. What kind of overall annual return on your investment do you feel is realistic?

10. What are your most important priorities at the present time?

Gaining Agreement to Take a Serious Look

You can move forward and make sale no. 3, Gaining Agreement to Take a Serious Look, only if

- A relationship of trust has been established
- A need has been recognized by the prospect
- A premium commitment has been decided upon

Assuming these conditions exist, we recommend that you say:

Rather than come to you today and tell you that you need this or that, quote you some prices, and sell you something on that basis, we at (company) in situations like yours do the opposite.

We ask you, "Have you made provisions in your life insurance and investment programs to maximize your monthly pension income when you retire? At your death, what sort of income do you want guaranteed to your family? What do you want done with the mortgage on your home if something happens to you? If you become sick or are injured, and can't work, what sort of income will you need? What sort of education do you want for your son and daughter?"

We take your responses to these and similar questions back to our office. There we study, analyze, and review your situation. With the assistance of our computer support, we individualize your case and personalize a recommendation for your consideration. In a few days, we return and give you our recommendation. If you like it, we'd like to have you as a client. However, you're under no obligation.

Now here is what I would like to do. (Lean forward and lower your voice) I'd like to gather this information. I'd like to pick up your policies. I'll take all of this to my office, where we will individualize your case. We will study your income and your obligations. We will review the insurance you already own and what it's doing for you. We will then prepare our personalized recommendation.

When I return, I'll give you some information and ideas that will be helpful to you now and in the future. No obligation, of course.

Now, (name), that's fair enough, isn't it? (Nod your head to assist your prospect in making a positive response).

Exhibit 3-4–Strategic Business Interview Questions

- How long have you been in business?
- Who started your business?
- What do you make or do?
- What is your net worth?
- How many people do you employ?
- Who owns your business?
- If more than one owner, what are their proportionate shares?
- Do you have a disability provision in your buy/sell?
- Is this a family business?
- Do you employ relatives and in what capacity?
- Will anybody be joining your company in the future?
- Do you have a salary continuation plan to provide for continuing income to disabled employees who are unable to work?
- How would you handle your own disability?
- What impact would your absence have on the corporation?
- How long and at what level would you continue your own salary?
- What provisions have you made to provide for this?
- When would you hire someone to take over?
- Other than yourself, is there someone so highly skilled or valuable that the loss would severely jeopardize your profitability?

- Draw me an organizational chart.
- Who are your key people? What are their incomes?
- How do you provide for them now?
- When would you have to hire a replacement? Who would you hire?
- Is there anyone in the company who could fill in temporarily?
- How long before someone new would become effective?
- How long could you afford to pay double salaries?
- When would you have to terminate the disabled employee?
- How would you improve on what you are presently doing?
- What other classifications of employees do you have? How do you provide for them? How would you improve on that?
- Do you or any of your key employees have any health problems?
- Request a census with birthdays, salaries, job descriptions, and known medical problems.
- Would you permit employees to buy or supplement their protection on a salary-allotment basis?
- What is most important to you?
- What would you like to do first? Second? Third?
- Would you like to see a way that you could do that?

Prudence A. Harker, CLU, ChFC
The Equitable Life Assurance Society
Beloit, Wisconsin

Record Data

Your next step is to gather full and complete information. Your company probably provides you the tool to use. If not, we recommend Brad Burkhart's Summit Client Information File. (See Appendix A). This is an integral part of the popular Summit Planning Process.

As you introduce the file, say to your prospect: "To do the best job possible for you, I'll need to record the information we have been discussing. Naturally, this will be held strictly confidential."

Obviously, there will be numerous situations where you will not find it practical or necessary to gather all of the information called for in this appendix.

The Money Commitment

To solidify your position, you must obtain a money commitment. We suggest this statement to ask for the commitment:

In your opinion, if you feel the recommendations we show you are logical in meeting your needs, how much could you set aside each month to accomplish your objectives?

When the prospect makes a money commitment, you have gained a definite and very positive sign of favorable action. This is why obtaining the money commitment is one of the most important elements of the entire selling process.

How You Strengthen the Commitment

It's the little things that count most in being an effective agent. Make it a practice to follow this strategic three-step procedure after you've gathered the necessary information. It will strengthen your case. As you conclude your first interview:

1. *Gather detailed medical information on a personal history blank and have it verified by the prospect.* Do this regardless of age. It helps you to solidify the case and also gives you valuable insights. For example, you may uncover a medical problem or find that you're facing competition. If so, take the prospect to your company's doctor and order out a policy from your underwriting department. *This will give you a definite competitive edge. The first completed medical almost always wins!*

2. *Next, you move forward to set up the next interview.* Let the time lapse between interviews be as short as possible and practical. Give the prospect an assurance such as:

> *We'll review thoroughly the information you gave me and your recommendation should be prepared within a week. Would a week from now be a convenient time to get together to show you our recommendation and go over it with you? Is the time we met today a convenient time, or would you prefer another? Let's plan to meet in my office, where we will be free from interruptions and where we have all the resource materials and computer assistance we might need.*

3. *Ask for two promises:*

> *I'd like you to promise me a couple of things. First, I'd like assurance from you that you will not consider a life insurance or equity purchase until I return with our recommendations for you.*

90

This indicates to your prospect that you feel he or she is a good prospect. Also, it secures for you the important obligation not to buy until you return.

Second, that when I return, you will study our personalized recommendations with an open mind and make your decisions at that time.

We encourage you to gain both of these commitments from your prospects. Do this until you have built a large clientele and have moved.

Deserve Your Prospect's Business

Only a thin line separates those who aspire to excellence in selling and those who attain it. Preparation is usually the quality that makes the difference. *Superior sales success is generally preceded by superior preparation.*

When the "qualifying interview" is completed, you have taken an important step toward making the "big sale." But you've taken only a step! Now you must generate an interest and strong feeling for (1) preparing your qualified prospect for the next step in the sales procedure, (2) preparing your recommendations, and (3) preparing yourself for the next interview.

According to the laws of cybernetics, the results you can expect from any sales presentation are pretty much in direct proportion to what you have contributed through your preparation. The preparation process helps you to use all of your selling equipment in an effort to deserve the buyer's business.

Preparing Your Prospect

Jack Murray, an outstanding agent and an active MDRT member from Detroit, sends out the type of letter shown in figure 3-4 on the day following his first interview.

After allowing time for the prospect to receive the letter, Jack calls to confirm the time and location of the next appointment. This letter does much to build a good relationship and to prepare the prospect for the

91

Figure 3-4

MURRAY FINANCIAL SERVICES, INC.

Chartered Financial Consultants

100 MAPLE PARK BOULEVARD, SUITE 135
ST. CLAIR SHORES, MICHIGAN 48081
(313) 774-9300 / 644-9200

September 1, 1988

Roger Green
13445 Saddle Lane
Grosse Point, Michigan 47391

Dear Roger:

It was good being with you and having the opportunity to discuss your life insurance situation with you. Thank you for allowing me the time to explain the professional procedure we use in our agency to help our many clients improve their financial position through the property of life insurance and equities. As I indicated, we are looking for clients we can serve at a profit—to them and to us.

In order that you might know a little more about our system of operation, I am taking the liberty of enclosing a brochure that gives you some background information and shows you the things we are doing to provide a complete life insurance and financial planning service for our many clients.

As we discussed, we will be prepared to present our recommendations to you on Monday, September 12, 1988. (Then Jack confirms the time and location of the next appointment.) By then the work that we do to individualize your case will have been completed.

Looking forward to seeing you then, I am

Yours sincerely,

Jack Murray, CLU

JM/laf

"buying interview." The brochure Jack mentions in his letter is attractive. It includes a code of ethics, some biographical background information, and his record of achievements, as well as a list of services he provides in the areas of personal and business insurance and employee-benefit plans.

Paving the Way

A key point to remember is that your prospect eventually will need to justify, either personally or to his or her company, the purchase made from you. Anything you can do to strengthen your position before you ask the prospect to buy is good psychology. Enclosing an appropriate article or brochure can be very effective in smoothing your path to the prospective client. But you must be selective in what you choose to send to the buyer. Most business and professional people today receive many such items every month. Very few items are carefully read unless they highlight a specific subject and can be immediately related, in a nontechnical manner, to one of the prospect's problems.

Whenever you see an interesting article, request permission to reprint it and have several copies made for your file. *Business Week, Nation's Business, Harvard Business Review, Fortune,* the *Wall Street Journal* and the *Executive Health Bulletin* have proved to be excellent sources of reprints for us.

Our associate in Dallas, Wally Smith, develops positive responses from prospects using the informational pieces shown in figure 3-5.

Possibly the best enclosures are reprints of articles you've written yourself for your company magazine and professional journals. These enhance your reputation and establish with the prospective buyer that you are a well-qualified agent.

Understand Buying Motives

What motivates one prospect to act on a certain suggestion may not be sufficient reason for another to do so. The prospect's desire to have your product, service, or idea springs from one or more basic motivations. *You must have a complete understanding of buying motives. You must be able*

Figure 3-5

Newspaper and magazine articles like these selected by Wally Smith of Dallas to be sent to his clients can be helpful in providing justification for the purchase of insurance. Such communication also help affirm your concern for the client's interests and well-being.

to determine the motives that are most likely to motivate each buyer, as well as which ones are most readily met by your suggestions.

Buying motives can be approached from two viewpoints: (1) the positive side, which is the prospect's impulse to gain something or to improve what he or she already has; and (2) the negative side, which is the fear of losing what he or she already possesses.

All of the lesser reasons for buying can be classified under the major headings that follow. Some prospects will buy because they want *monetary gain* they receive today from interest-sensitive policies and from universal, variable-life products, and equity products. They want to profit from and add to their money values. Others are principally interested in *preventing financial loss*. These are the prospects who are buying protection from you.

Prospects often buy what you sell because of *love of family, love of self, or love of charity.* They buy because of *fear of loss by death or disability.* Prospects may buy because of a *tax advantage.* Their motivation might be *pride of ownership.* At times, they are even motivated to buy because *someone they know and respect made the decision to buy from you.*

There is *always* a motive behind the buyer's decision to take action on your recommendations. You position yourself by uncovering the motive and focusing on it.

How Your Buyer Buys

Positioning assists the prospect in making certain decisions in your favor, one decision at a time. When your prospect has made them all, he or she has bought your product or service. But what is the buying process? How does the buyer buy? The buyer buys by making the following four decisions:

1. I will listen to this agent.
2. I recognize I have a need.
3. I will look at a solution.
4. I will act now.

These four different but important decisions must be reached by the prospect, and they do so in a logical, orderly manner.

95

Why Your Buyer Buys

The buyer buys because he or she likes *you*, the agent. Research reveals that favorable feelings toward the agent are the principal reason the buyer buys, becomes a client, and makes referrals. Therefore, throughout your career, you must constantly learn more and better ways of making good first impressions and building relationships.

Another reason the buyer buys is because he or she sees and understands a definite "owner benefit." In addition, the buyer buys because you have assisted him or her in making each of the buying decisions. In a very real sense, you must play the role of being an "assistant buyer."

Positioning facilitates the process of turning prospects into clients. Positioning encourages centers of influence to function effectively for you. When you position yourself appropriately to prospects, clients, and centers of influence, you improve your chances for financial success in today's competitive marketplace.

Chapter Three Flashbacks

1. Positioning is defined as getting in front of _decision makers_ and creating _selling climate_ that encourage action on your recommendations.
2. Positioning begins with _making favorable 1st impressio_
3. It's important to decide how you want to be _perceived_ by your prospects and clients.
4. _Paying attention_ is identified as a way to consistently increase your production.
5. Prospecting becomes as natural as breathing for you when you consistently _pay attention_ and maintain an _action file_.
6. Telephone success requires you to do three things:
   a. Always have a _reason_ for calling.
   b. Follow a _prepared script_.
   c. Be _brief_.
7. Your approach to the first interview has two objectives:
   a. To make a _favorable impression_ upon your prospect.
   b. To arouse _positive interest_.
8. You'll learn to cope with call reluctance and to build call courage when you follow these suggestions:
   a. Stay _sold_ on what you are selling.
   b. Saturate your mind with _mental oil_.
   c. Prepare yourself _technically_.
   d. Focus on the _rewards of success_.
   e. Remind yourself that most people are _nice_ people.
   f. Let prospects key off of your _attitude_ —never key off of your prospects'.
9. The one thing all of your prospects have in common is the need to be _appreciated_. "Ego food" is a powerful substance to use in building relationships, providing it's _believable_.
10. Research reveals _you_ are the principal reason the buyer _buys_, becomes a client, and refers others. You must play the role of being an " _assistant buyer_"

For answers see page 231.

97

Self-Motivators for Creating the Selling Climate

Remember that success in making a sale depends not on your prospect, but on *you*—on how you think, feel, and act. W. Clement Stone's story at the beginning of this chapter about how he conditioned his mind to sell in Sioux Center demonstrates the use of self-motivators in creating a selling climate. You can use them, too:

Success is achieved by those who try and maintained by those who keep trying with PMA.

There is an intelligent solution to any problem if you keep your mind on what you want and off what you don't want.

Pay attention!

As you condition your mind to develop mental readiness for each call, remember to:

Stay sold on what you are selling.

Prepare yourself technically.

Focus on building relationships of trust.

In making use of the telephone as a business tool, keep this self-motivator in mind:

Successful telephone contacts are made by those who develop tele-confidence with PMA.

I don't know what your destiny will be. But, one thing I do know: the only ones among you who will be really happy are those who have sought and found how to serve.

—Albert Schweitzer

Commentary: An Organized Sales Talk Spells Success

A successful sales formula is similar to an intricate mathematical equation: the whole is made up of all its parts, and the parts may comprise several steps or related formulas. It is important to realize this because in developing an organized sales talk, you may be close to finding your formula without recognizing that you lack a few essential parts, or even one small step, to make it complete.

Ten Essential Ingredients

Bear in mind that there are ten essentials of an effective sales talk:

1. *Use a good introduction.* Everything must have a beginning. The purpose of the introduction is to get the prospect to listen and to arouse his interest.

2. *Concentrate the prospect's attention.* If the item is small, let the prospect actually hold it; if it is large, get him to concentrate his attention on specific points of interest; if it's an intangible, actually look at the literature yourself while pointing to the sentence or illustration, thus using the directional force of your own eyes to get the prospect to also look at that to which you are pointing.

3. *Relieve tension.* You want your prospect to like you, so smile. If you can get him to laugh at effective humor, you relieve tension within him as well as neutralize timidity on your own part.

4. *Use enthusiasm.* If you talk in a sincere, enthusiastic manner, you will appeal to your prospect's emotions and accelerate your own enthusiasm.

5. *Ask questions.* You can direct your prospect's mind in the desired channel by asking him specific questions that require answers other than a yes or no reflex answer. If, of course, you want a series of yes answers, then ask questions that make it easy for your prospect to answer yes.

6. *Give a complete description.* Explain in full the advantage of your service or product. If time is short, use as few words as possible (this requires planning and practice). Be honest, and employ the golden rule.

7. *Use colorful words and phrases.* The use of adjectives and descriptive phrases helps romance a talk that might otherwise be dull.

8. *Use influential names.* Persons buy what people buy, and people buy what persons buy. The use of influential names reduces sales resistance and helps arouse interest as well as close sales. By influential, we mean the use of names that will influence the prospect, not necessarily that the names need be so-called "big names." For example, on Milwaukee Avenue in Chicago, the name of the merchant next door is by far more influential than that of the president of the United States or the president of a bank in New York.

In an establishment of any size, the name of the employer in that particular firm generally carries more weight and influence than outside names. In any vocation or profession, the names of persons in that same field have influence. The name of a relative or friend, regardless of his or her financial status, carries a great deal of weight.

9. *Show something.* Brochures, pictured illustrations, samples of the merchandise, or other visual aids often clearly picture in the prospect's mind the type of product or service that you are selling. Therefore, these can and should, in many instances, be used. Show something! The physical handling of these selling aids is important. If you want a person to look at an object that can't be handled physically, you don't need to ask the

100

person to take it—all you need to do is hand it over. If you want a person to read something, place the material in a position that will make it easy for him or her to read; don't present a document upside down or at an angle.

10. *Use an effective close*. Everything must have an ending. Agents who are not in the large income brackets are generally those who do not close.

A well-organized sales talk would probably have a standard close and one or two additional closes to be used, if necessary, after rebuttal arguments.

If you are already selling a product or service, it should not be difficult to develop a successful, organized sales talk. Be alerted to the reaction of your prospects in your use of each of the ten essentials. That which develops favorable reaction should be employed regularly; that which doesn't, eliminate.

—*W. Clement Stone*

Chapter Four
The Power of Persuasiveness
Making More And Better Sales

A sales rep who can't close sales that don't close themselves, who can't direct prospects' thoughts into proper channels and overcome their tendency to procrastinate, isn't a sales rep at all. He or she is merely a conversationalist.

—Charles Roth

The Most Important Factor

Confidence is the single most important factor in making sales. It's not the prospect. It's not the computerized printout. It's not the interest rate or business conditions. It's *you* the agent—the "key player"—the person who assists the buyer in making the decision to act *now*. And how do you assist the buyer in this way? By being confident enough to make the prospect feel confident in what you are recommending.

Let's face it—confidence is the fuel that powers persuasiveness. Without it you do not sell; you just take orders. And where does confidence come from? It is the product of preparation and knowledge.

To be sure, there are myriad products you are selling today that are new and different—all the way from low-cost annual renewable term to vanishing-premium, universal, variable-life, and equity products. But the principles by which these modern plans are sold are still the age-old principles of *consultative selling* which are detailed in this chapter.

The ability to persuade and to close sales is still the most important factor in any agent's career. *The fundamental principle of the close is that you must be persuasive and tell your prospect that you want him or her to act now on your recommendation.* If you hesitate in doing this, if you hold back, if you are timid, if you are vague, you may have many pleasant interviews each week, but you will seldom have any sales. Even though you handle every other step of the selling process perfectly, your approach will flop unless you climax it with a persuasive presentation and strong closing actions.

Preparing the Recommendation

Successful sales interviews begin with preparation. As you prepare the presentation, remember the promise you've made to individualize and personalize the prospect's case. This is a major responsibility. It's one of the most important of all the steps in successful selling because it requires you to adopt your prospect's point of view. Make your proposals distinctive. They should show evidence of thought and preparation. An example of how a proposal can be made distinctive is illustrated by the popular MDRT past president, Wilmer Poynor III. Wilmer prepares four mock checks for his prospects. The first check is for the amount of the death benefit payable to the beneficiary. The second, made out to the prospect, represents the cash build-up payable at age sixty-five. The third check, also in the prospect's name, is for the total of monthly lifetime retirement income payable, beginning at age sixty-five.

And the fourth check? It's made out to New York Life, Wilmer's company, in the amount of the monthly premium. Wilmer then says to his prospect: "Now to make these first three checks possible, this is the check I need from you each month."

You can make selling life insurance as complicated or as simple as you want. Using Wilmer's technique, when your prospect looks at the benefits being in the hundreds of thousands of dollars, and the premium, which is always relatively very small, you've painted a very appealing and persuasive picture.

Your recommendation won't produce a sale unless it is built around the prospect's interest. People never buy insurance or equity products unless they feel it's in their best interest to do so. This is why you must be prepared to convince the prospect of the ways in which your recommendations will be beneficial to his or her family, company, or favorite charity. Review and study the information you gathered from your prospective buyer to determine what he or she needs and wants to accomplish. Then develop your recommendation in a way that convinces your prospect that your product offers the best way to solve those personal needs and reach personal goals.

Do you want to make the sale? Then design the program that you would buy if you had your prospect's needs, desires, and problems (and, if you do, the program you had better already own).

Build What You Would Want

A builder had become wealthy, partly through the efforts of his capable foreman. One day as he was about to go on vacation, he called the foreman and asked him to build a house while he was gone. "Choose the lot that you like best and build the house exactly as you would like it," he said.

The builder left on vacation, and the foreman picked out a lot and began construction. But he was disgruntled about having this new assignment added to his work load. So he cut corners in building the new house—nothing anyone could see—but shortcuts, nonetheless. "After all," the foreman thought, "the boss will never know."

When the builder returned from his vacation, the house was completed. He and the foreman walked through it together. As they were leaving, the builder locked the front door, turned to the foreman, and handed him the keys, saying, "I'm grateful for all the fine work you've done for me. This is your house."

"Build your own house" every time you build for someone else. Give the prospect exactly what you would want, what you would be willing to buy for the amount that you are suggesting that he or she pay. *You can't be truly confident in what you are proposing to a prospect if you don't believe it is what you would want yourself.* And if you do believe, then how can you be less than absolutely confident?

Anticipate Objections

Once you're convinced, however, you must anticipate your prospect's objections. What are the problems he or she might have in buying that could preclude acting now? For one thing, *determine how your prospect is going to pay the premium.* Most prospects won't object to owning the additional life-insurance or equity products you recommend, but they may object to the financial outlay it requires. If you leave the problem of finding the required dollars up to your prospect, you're leaving him or her with the most difficult job of all. It's usually unreasonable of you to expect the prospect to work it out. *So you must determine for the prospect how the premium can be paid;* perhaps by transferring capital from some other asset, or by use of accumulated dividends, eliminating corporate dividends, using an annual bonus, or any of a number of other ways.

Preparing Yourself

No matter how long a show plays on Broadway, the actors continue to rehearse. They are professionals and they conscientiously seek perfection. They practice their lines and their every move, because each has a particular purpose. They know exactly what they are saying. They understand the response and reaction they must receive from their audience.

Preparation means being so well-organized that you know before you make your presentation that the prospect will buy your recommendation. You can anticipate some objections; you should prepare yourself to answer them before they are expressed.

Call a day or two in advance to confirm the appointment tentatively set in your previous interview. You'll want to say something like this:

(Name), I have the recommendations I promised we would develop for you. We had agreed upon (day) at (time) in (place) as the best time for us to get together. Is that still convenient for you?

Make sure the prospect can be there at the designated time. Be certain that all the dominant parties will be present. By dominant parties, we mean those who have a part in the decision to buy and pay for your recommendation, for example, a spouse or a business partner. *You don't want to give your presentation for practice.*

Be sure you have all the essential materials with you for the interview. These will include your papers from the opening interview, the prospect's file and application forms, as well as the policies you picked up during the first meeting.

The Prepared Mind

It's not what you propose or what you say to your prospect that counts, it's what he or she accepts. Acceptance depends on the quantity and quality of your preparation.

Then, too, when you're convinced that what you're recommending is the best and most logical course of action for the prospect to take, your mind is clear. It's clear to make important observations, to answer any questions, to meet any objections. It gives you the confidence that nothing you will encounter in the interview can detour you. Moreover, as a result of the thoroughness of your preparation, you are aware that clients' families will be better protected; their financial goals are going to be met; their businesses are more likely to be preserved.

The Planned Presentation

While there is probably no single, best way to present your recommendation, we strongly encourage you to follow a planned format. Do this regardless of the kind of insurance involved, the size of the policy, or the amount of the premium. Following set patterns in the buying interview does not deny you the use of your personality. It doesn't prevent you from displaying your natural abilities. In fact, it does just the opposite. It frees you to be more natural since you are not preoccupied with the myriad details that must be covered, you have already mastered them, internalized them, made them part of your format.

A planned format makes it possible for you to devote your thinking, when under the pressure of the interview, to the "post-graduate" facets of selling, such as listening and interpreting the prospect's nonverbal language. For example, by carefully watching the prospect's actions you can learn things that might never be said aloud. Body language can tell you if the prospect is receptive, reluctant, pleased, puzzled, disbelieving, uncertain, or convinced. But you won't have a chance to notice these nonverbals if you're busy thinking about what to say and do next. *To sell at your best, you must become a good "eye-listener."* You can do this only after you have mastered a set selling procedure and learned your lines. This is the reason that a great agent like Frank Sullivan of Mutual Benefit in New Jersey, says, "Ad-libs are for amateurs."

Essentials of an Effective Presentation

Your effectiveness as an agent will always be measured by the number of satisfied clients you develop. Prior to making your presentations, you invest many hours and successfully "make several sales" in the client-building process. The earlier "sales" in the process are important but they lead nowhere if you can't sell your recommendations and persuade prospects to act *now.*

Your presentation must be designed from the buyer's point of view. In other words, it must give the kind of information your prospect wants and needs to have before he or she is willing to buy. It must make the prospect understand, agree with, and act upon your recommendations. Knowing how to develop and deliver a convincing presentation is one of the surest and quickest ways to reach the top of your company's honor roll.

Some companies give you a prepared sales script and insist that you learn to give it verbatim. Others leave it up to you to plan and develop your own sales talk. Whatever the practice of your company, and no matter what kind of product you are trying to sell, it's necessary for you to thoroughly understand the four essentials of a result-producing presentation if you are to sell effectively:

1. It must capture your prospect's instant and undivided attention.
2. It must arouse interest by describing owner benefits and their advantages to the prospect. (The problem must be made clear, with

108

the implication that without your solution it will remain an urgent and ever-present problem.)

3. It must build desire by winning your prospect's confidence.
4. It must motivate your prospect to take action now.

Proven Presentation Principles

Whether or not your prospect is willing to buy depends largely on his or her internal feelings during your presentation. *These feelings are strongly influenced by the prospect's perception of what you say and do, how you act, and whether or not you are perceived as being trustworthy.* Therefore, you must form the habit of saying and doing those things that create a perception that you are trustworthy and professional.

Let's examine twelve proven presentation principles. Study these carefully. Make them a dominant part of your presentation strategy.

1. *Build credibility.* This starts with preparation. You should have already developed enough information to be fully convinced that what you recommend is truly in the prospect's best interest. *Demonstrate, as early as possible, a sincere interest in the prospect as a person.* Build the trust level quickly. Use referrals up front whenever you can. The fact that other people who are respected by the prospect have found you trustworthy creates the impression that you are trustworthy. Convey the impression that you expect to be believed and trusted. Don't say or do anything that might annoy or offend the prospect.

2. *Be well-mannered.* Liberal use of phrases such as, "May I ask . . . ," or, "If it's all right with you . . . ," "Let's . . . ," tend to win the confidence of the prospect. They will build your image as a mature, likable agent.

3. *Simplify your suggestions.* The power of your recommendations will always lie in their simplicity. And simplicity always lies in comprehensive knowledge and thorough preparation.

4. *Speak the prospect's language.* Stay away from industry jargon. Keep your explanations simple as you focus on "owner benefits."

5. *Speak as one having authority.* Develop a "lean on me" environment. Show enthusiasm for your suggestions. Human emotions

are highly transferable. Look and speak in terms of success. Prospects like to buy from agents they perceive as being successful.

6. *Sell at the buyer's pace.* Be willing to let the prospect interrupt you—but never interrupt the prospect. Interrupting implies that you have something more important to say. You are not the most important person in the room, your prospect is. And the prospect can sense whether you understand this or not. That's why successful selling is an unselfish activity. So make the buyer feel the truth of his or her importance, and you'll make the sale.

7. *Avoid overstatement.* It implies that the prospect is naive. It can also result in disbelief in anything else you say.

8. *Avoid dogmatic statements.* Skillful agents say, "Many of our clients have found it best to . . . ," and, "Others have said . . . ," instead of, "The only sound way to do this is . . ."

9. *Use repetition.* Repetition overcomes communication difficulties. Try to make your meaning clear by giving more details, by furnishing examples, and by making analogies. *Repeated assertion is hard to resist.* The initial reaction of the human mind is to reject anything new. This natural, instinctive reaction is a healthy one because it causes the prospect to think of the pros and cons of the idea and to avoid impulsive decisions he or she might later regret. However, if something is repeated over and over, the prospect's "natural defenses" tend to weaken because the idea is no longer "new." The tendency is to then admit that "it might be a good idea," and the prospect moves closer to acceptance.

10. *Make it the prospect's idea.* Each of us is best convinced by reasons we discover for ourselves. Be judged an expert without "flaunting" your knowledge. Avoid even the slightest appearance of feeling superior to the prospect.

11. *Summarize strategically.* "Let's examine again . . ." Cement the owner benefits. Make certain you have gained understanding.

12. *Close with confidence.* Master and perfect your strategy for securing action on your recommendations. Close by assuming. Close by assisting the buyer. Help the prospect to make the all-important decision to buy.

We suggest that you review these presentation principles frequently. They go to the heart of the process the prospect moves through in deciding whether or not to buy what you are recommending.

The Effective Agent *ASKS*

The secret of closing more sales is to make certain your prospect understands precisely and clearly what you are saying. *Understanding is the first secret of closing more and better sales.*

The importance of understanding cannot be overrated. It is the reason we say that the power of your presentation lies in its simplicity.

A confused prospect seldom becomes a buyer, so make everything clear as you move along; a prospect will rarely admit that he or she doesn't understand what you've been saying. Clear, simple language carries the most conviction. You want the prospect to fully understand your recommendation and to feel that he or she has made the decision to buy. However, to effectively move the prospect to take action, the effective agent always *ASKS,* an acronym we use for Attract, Stimulate, Know, and Summarize:

- *Attract your prospect's attention.* Review with the prospect the minutes of your "qualifying interview." Use the Confidential Data Form that you completed in the previous interview and go through it point by point in complete detail. This review gains attention and brings your prospect to the same level of thinking and emotion as he or she was at the conclusion of the first interview. *During your review, attempt to overcome any objections you think might come up later in the interview.* Repeat aloud the positive statements your prospect made to you during the earlier interview. This will amplify and reinforce the prospect's original opinions and feelings.

- *Stimulate your prospect's interest.* Recapitulate client needs and explain the role insurance and equities play in every person's financial picture. Show how your products can enhance the prospect's personal portfolio. Focus on "owner benefits." Say, for example:

111

My company has molded its many years of insurance and investment experience into the development of this modern-day consumer-oriented plan we are recommending.

Our plan has been constructed on a flexible basis and it will do three things for you, (name) and (name).

First of all, it will guarantee you that money will be accumulated and available for you at the time when it is wanted and needed most. It provides lifetime protection against death for a premium that does not increase as you grow older.

Second, the plan guarantees a buildup of cash values, which will be available for you at retirement or to supply needed cash in the interim to allow you to take advantage of opportunities or meet with an unexpected financial problem.

Third, our plan is responsive to changes in interest rates. As interest rates climb, both your protection and cash benefits respond and go up, too. In other words, your policy values benefit from (company's) investment portfolio. Of course, interest rates can go down, too. (How you describe this plan benefit depends upon the design of your company's contract).

In this manner, you describe in simple terms how life insurance is the purchase of dollars for future delivery. Bear in mind this prospect's particular "hot button," which you discovered in the previous interview. Arouse buying motives: point out that your recommended plan will guarantee that dollars to fulfill your prospect's financial objectives will be accumulated and available at the time they're wanted and needed most. *Keeping your prospect's objectives in focus sharpens the appetite and makes him or her anxious to hear more.* It's an important step in the closing format. It must be carefully planned and then executed with conviction and confidence.

- *Know you're understood.* Move from the general approach of the preceding step into specifics by explaining your proposal. Present the facts and figures, remembering to keep your presentation simple. Since your prospect is probably unfamiliar with proposals and with most insurance terminology, don't rush. Instead, gain understanding by amplifying the basics of your recommendation, one step at a time.

One of the ways you'll know you are understood is by listening—with both your ears and your eyes. Watch for signs that indicate confusion, or disinterest, or even antagonism. Don't be afraid to stop and change the subject in order to clear the prospect's mind. If he or she is not listening, it doesn't matter what you say in your presentation, or how well you say it, it will not be heard. So keep "listening" with those three ears Ben Feldman talked about. This is the only way to make sure your prospect is listening, too.

Obtain consent by occasionally punctuating with questions such as: "Isn't that right?" and "What's your opinion?" And such statements as: "You, yourself, have said . . . " and, "As you probably would point out . . ."

Discuss the required premium throughout your presentation rather than surprising the prospect with the amount at the end. Moreover, keep the application visible so you won't have to reach for it later, possibly making the prospect shy away when it suddenly appears.

Along with premiums, discuss the extra features you recommend. Such features as disability waiver, accidental death, and the option to purchase additional insurance can help make the sale. You might introduce them this way:

We recommend disability premium waiver as a part of this plan. When you are sick or hurt and can't work for six months, your premium will be discontinued until the disability stops. During the period of disability, the values in your policy keep building and the regular dividends will keep coming just as if you were paying the regular premium.

We usually recommend the accidental death benefit, which, if you die from an accident, will pay an additional amount equal to the face amount of the policy.

Another important feature of this plan is the option to purchase additional insurance, which assures that you'll have the opportunity to own more life insurance in the future—even if a change in health would normally make you ineligible.

- *Summarize*. Now, emphasize the three main things the plan will do for this person: whether he or she lives to retirement without any extraordinary financial need, does incur such a financial need, or dies before accomplishing his or her financial goals. Stress the flexibility of the plan: it will accomplish your prospect's financial objectives no matter what. Again, make sure the plan is understood and that your prospect's questions are answered. *Understanding is the key!* Remember, if everyone truly understood life insurance, prospects would be knocking at your office door to get some. As it is, your job as an agent is really that of being an educator. Once you make your prospect *understand* how your recommendations guarantee his or her reaching cherished financial goals, *the purchase of your plan represents the best choice.*

The Closing Strategy

Clint Davidson, in his book *How I Discovered the Secret of Success in the Bible*, said: *First, you must get a person's favorable attention. Then you must change that attention into interest in the thing you want to do. Third, you must build the interest until it becomes desire. Finally, you must change desire into action."* This is precisely the strategy we recommend that you use.

Remember, most insurance sales do not close themselves. You must do the closing. Nothing is more important during this part of the selling process than your confidence, born of thorough preparation in the time-proven five-step strategy for closing.

Step 1—Summarize

We feel, and we think you'll agree, (name), that my company has developed this program for (spouse) and you on a very flexible basis, and that it will do for you the things you want done by your life insurance program.

114

First, this plan guarantees you that money will be accumulated and available for future delivery when you become too old to work.

Second, our plan provides a guaranteed monthly income to (spouse) and your family at your death.

Finally, the plan provides an accumulation of funds available for financial opportunities or contingencies in the years ahead.

Step 2 — Ask for prospect's questions and apply silence

I want to be certain both of you understand our recommendation. Give this a final look and see if there are any questions that either of you have that I haven't already answered.

Place the proposal in front of your prospect. Make it possible for him or her to show positive buying signs. Keep quiet, listen and watch for opportunities to encourage and reinforce your prospect's "discoveries," realizations regarding various facets of your plan's owner benefits. At the same time, position the application and an uncapped pen in front of you. *You're asking the prospect to give your recommendation a final look.* Ask him or her to check the names for correct spelling and see if there are any questions yet to be answered.

Then let silence go to work for you. To use silence requires courage and practice. Be aware that the proper application of silence can do much to help you close sales.

In some cases, you'll receive a buying signal; in most cases, you won't. You'll have to assist your prospects in making the decision. This requires that you continue with the five-step closing strategy, which you will have practiced and perfected. Already you have handled the first two steps: summarizing the benefits of the plan, then asking for the prospect's questions and using silence.

Step 3 — Ask two opinion questions — (trial closes)

If you have no further questions, (name), there are two questions I'd like to ask you and (spouse). The first is about the plan itself. In your opinion, do you feel that our plan does for you the things you want done by an insurance/investment plan?

This is a controlled question. By that, we mean the response you'll receive is predictable. This question almost invariably gets a favorable response.

When you receive the prospect's nod and approval of the plan, immediately move your eyes from the prospect to the application and record the name of the plan on the application. Then proceed by saying:

The second question is this: what about the amount we are recommending? Do you feel it's about right—an amount you'll be comfortable with, (name), based upon your current budget and the dollars you have available to invest that we discussed earlier?

When you refer to the amount, you mean either the premium or the volume. You'll often meet some resistance in asking about the amount. However, you positioned yourself to close the sale when you received the initial favorable response to your plan and you began to write on the app. Now, your prospect must stop you, or he or she is giving you consent to fix up the app. *Again, the important attitude to develop and maintain is that the sale must be closed; it seldom closes itself.*

Step 4—Stimulate action with minor decision questions

Let's assume you resolved the amount decision. You then record the amount on the application. Next, you move to secure consent on a number of minor questions, shifting your prospect's attention to little decisions. In effect, you're now giving control of the idea to take action on your recommendation to the prospect, making it the prospect's idea. You can say:

(Name), would you prefer to handle the premium annually or on our monthly check-o-matic?

Would you like to receive your correspondence here at your business or at your home?

Again, you record the response on the application. *People love to buy but are reluctant to be sold. In this step, you are letting the prospect buy when he or she responds to the choices you offer.* You can ask about the beneficiary arrangement, additional features, such as the option to purchase additional insurance, waiver of premium, and accidental death. In each instance, you give your prospect a choice. *On each of these minor points you continue to acknowledge both actual response and implied consent by recording them on the application.* Let your prospect buy!

Step 5 — Ask prospect to write name on application and give you a check

Next, you mark an X on the application next to the signature line and hand your prospect the pen. You then say:

Put your name right here, (name), if you will, please.

Never ask your prospect to *sign* an application. Most Americans have been taught since an early age never to sign anything, but they will "write their name" on almost anything.

After the app is signed, you move ahead with this statement:

(Name), please make your check for $1,027, payable to (company).

Next in importance to the early minutes of the initial contact is the time when you ask for the check for the initial premium. This should be done in a very matter-of-fact manner.

You are now properly positioned to complete the application in its entirety. This is a simple thing to get done after you have the app signed and the check for the initial premium.

Words With Special Power

Effective closers weigh every expression. They always try to use words that will be acceptable — words that will have positive, rather than negative, impact in the prospect's mind. *You want a "yes" response, so keep your prospect in a frame of mind in which he or she will agree, rather than disagree, with what you say. Keep them answering, "yes, yes, yes," and you keep them buying.*

A few key words have extraordinary power to influence people (see exhibit *4-1*). One of these is the word *why*. *Why* is one of the hardest of all questions for the prospect to answer without making a commitment. Learn to use *why* and you will draw out the real reason your prospect is hesitant to sign the application.

Let's is a useful word in closing sales because it implies mutuality. "Let's move forward on this basis," makes the prospects feel it's as much their idea as it is yours, and motivates them to cooperate. Another word with motivation strength is *how*. When New York Life's Ray Triplett says, "I'm going to show you *how* to make deductible gifts to your grandchildren in such a way that they will never forget you," he arouses a sense of curiosity. Prospects want to hear the rest.

Receiving Valuable Feedback

This is one of the most widely discussed topics in the field of selling. For the inexperienced agent, the skeptical tone of a prospect's objection is too often interpreted as a refusal to buy. In the face of objections, the rhythm of a presentation is broken, self-confidence wavers, and conviction is often lost.

Two factors will determine your success in meeting resistance and overcoming objections: attitude and strategy. As with any part of the selling process, strategy can be learned and mastered through practice. But, first, it's important to develop an attitude that puts objections in their proper perspective.

All too often, objections are viewed as major obstacles to closing the sale. *When you develop skill in handling them, you'll find objections are a welcome part of the sales process.* In fact, often the toughest prospect to sell is the one who gives you too little or no feedback. It's hard to tell where he or she stands. The same applies to the prospect who appears to agree with everything you say. For these reasons, the right attitude toward objections is to welcome them. *Objections provide a clue to your prospect's thought process.* Early in the sales presentation you fish for feedback to determine the prospect's thoughts and feelings about the points being presented. You welcome this as useful information. When a prospect provides an objection, this is valuable feedback, too. *You're getting direct thoughts about your recommendation.* Objections can serve you well if you learn to welcome them and if you have the strategy for handling them.

Once you have the right attitude toward objections, you can develop a strategy for handling them effectively. But to do so, you must first determine whether they are genuine or insincere. The insincere objection,

Exhibit 4-1—Powerful Expressions

Words That Probe

Why?
How?
What is your opinion?
What do you think?
Can you illustrate?
What do you consider?
What were the circumstances?
How do you feel about...?
Could you explain?
Which would be best for you?

Words That Motivate

Thank you	Flexible
Congratulations!	Value
Let's	Profit
I would appreciate your courtesy	Love
I want to make certain I understand how you feel.	God
Will you help me?	Guarantee
It was my fault.	Safe
I'm proud of you!	Loss
Please	Qualify
You were very kind.	Home
It's been a real pleasure.	Recommend
Growth	Up-to-date
Quality	Death

Words That Irritate

Understand?
Get the point?
Do you see what I mean?
To be honest with you
Bucks
Deal
I, me, my, mine
I'll tell you what!
You know

known as sales resistance, is generally illogical and cannot be answered. It's expressed in alibis, excuses, or stalls. The prospect may give you fictitious reasons to hide the real, genuine objection—for example, "I'm tied up at the office right now, I just don't have the time"; "Your plan has a lot of merit, but I'd like to think about it"; "I'd like to shop around and do some comparing."

By contrast, the genuine objection has the ring of truthfulness. Here, the prospect feels there's a valid reason for not buying at this time. Examples: "The need is an obvious one, but I have some bills I have to handle first"; "Frankly, I feel as though I can invest my money better in my own business"; "It's just too expensive for me right now, there's no way I can afford it."

These objections are not excuses. They are genuine doubts in the prospect's mind, and you can handle them. As you gain experience, it will become easier for you to distinguish between genuine and insincere objections. Eventually you'll have heard them all. Like an actor in a long-running play, you'll soon know not only your lines but the lines of all the other performers as well.

No matter how skillful you become at anticipating and answering objections before they come up, some will still surface. *When they do, handle them in one of three ways: ignore, defer, or answer them.*

Since most people tend to react defensively early in a buying situation, it's best to manage initial resistance by ignoring it completely. In other words, don't try to counter it with logic. Maintain your poise and build the prospect's confidence by displaying empathy and patience. Say something like, "I can understand how you feel," or, "That's all right," and then move ahead confidently to ask for the appointment, adding: "I would appreciate very much your courtesy in giving me thirty minutes—just thirty minutes—to show you the kind of work we are doing for our clients today." You'll find this an effective way to chase early resistance.

The second way of handling an objection is to defer it by simply asking permission to answer it later. When you delay an objection during the presentation, you rob it of some of its potential strength. Also, the delay keeps you on track. Best of all, delaying an objection often tables it permanently.

As you move to the closing of your presentation and a genuine objection surfaces, you must answer it to the prospect's satisfaction. To hesitate or be evasive may magnify the objection in the prospect's mind and block the close. *The sense of personal selling power derived from confidence in having a strategy for handling objections is an invaluable asset.* Once your strategy is mastered, you'll be able to remain poised and react calmly when confronted with objections.

A Six-Step Strategy

Any genuine objection can be handled successfully by following, step-by-step, the strategy outlined below:

1. *Hear the prospect out.* There should be no knee-jerk responses, no quick moves. Never interrupt the prospect, even when you know what is coming and have a response in mind. *Be encouraged that the objection is being voiced; it is evidence that your prospect is listening and thinking.* It means you have more selling to do, but it also points the way. An objection focuses attention on those areas where the prospect requires more information and understanding. Listening to the objection establishes empathy. How you listen is important. Lean forward, let your facial expression register "I'm taking your objection seriously."

2. *Ask the prospect to repeat the objection, whenever you feel it's appropriate.* This shows you are taking the objection seriously. Say, "I want to be certain that I understand how you feel. May I ask you to repeat your thought?" This returns the ball to the prospect's court. Quite often, when asked to repeat, a prospect will give you a new, completely different objection. Or, he or she may restate it in such a way that it's easier for you to handle. Sometimes, repeating even causes the prospect to realize his or her objection is groundless. In any event, by hearing it out, then asking for a restatement, you allow the prospect to take part in the closing in a very meaningful, cooperative way.

3. *Restate the objection.* This does several things for you. It tells the prospect you have been listening and that you understand what was said. Also, it makes it clear that you don't accept the objection as being final. It gives you time to reorganize your thoughts, and this can be helpful. *The restating step puts you in step with the prospect.* It will help you avoid arguments. Remember, there's probably more inclination to indulge in ar-

guments when answering questions or objections than in any other part of the interview. No one ever convinced a prospect by arguing, so *stay in the prospect's corner.* Guide him or her to better understanding by providing more information. Do this by tackling the objection, not the prospect.

4. *Isolate the objection.* This helps you decide if this is the *only* objection, as well as the *real* objection. There are always two reasons a prospect has for not deciding upon your recommendation: the reason that sounds good, and the real reason. You must smoke out the real reason by saying, "In addition to that, would there be any other reason you might have for not acting on our recommendation today?"

5. *Use an illustration, example, or story.* More objections are overcome by emotional responses than through intellectual appeals. You can educate prospects on the soundness of your plan, and you can get them nodding affirmatively at every point. But, until you stir them emotionally, there's likely to be no action. Carefully selected illustrations and stories exert tremendous power over the prospect's mind. Let them see themselves in the light of another person's experience. Each of us tends to identify with the main character in a story, so if relevant examples are given, the prospect will identify with the hero, or the goat. Several power phrases and sample motivational stories are given at the conclusion of this chapter.

6. *Assist the prospect in taking action.* The only reason for answering an objection is to complete the sale. Properly executed, the first five steps have moved your prospect into a position where it is more reasonable for him or her to say yes than to say no.

Again, the most important factor in stimulating action is your confidence. *Always assume your prospect is going to buy now.* Proceed as if all you must do is settle the few questions of minor importance. Your attitude can make closing the sale easy and natural. Don't be argumentative. This is not always an easy thing to accomplish, especially when your prospect clings to an objection. *Learn to defend your plan without being defensive.* Remember, you are doing all this for your prospect. Your prospect just doesn't know it until you allow him or her to understand. So be patient, teacher. No student ever learns if he or she feels questions can't be asked. That's all any prospect's objections are: unanswered questions.

Handling Last-Minute Objections

When you encounter genuine objections near the close of your presentation, whatever the substance of your prospect's objection, he or she is really saying, "I'm not sold, at least not yet." There are three basic reasons for this.

1. *There is something that is not understood.* You must do a better job of explaining your recommendation in relation to the prospect's needs or desires.
2. *There is something the prospect does not believe.* You have not produced sufficient evidence to convince the prospect of the true benefits and value of your proposal.
3. *An objection may mean there is something the prospect is trying to cover up.* When you sense this, you must be considerate. Try to build confidence and reduce the prospect's anxiety.

Prospects will follow you willingly on those things that happen to be in accord with their own desires. However, they must be *directed, assisted,* and *persuaded* if you are to get the action and cooperation you desire for their benefit.

Some people who seemingly should buy, simply will not. On the other hand, some prospects will buy despite their own objections. Why? Because they discover a reason for buying that exerts more pressure and influence than any of the negative reasons.

In today's sophisticated, fast-changing marketplace, prospects look to you for information and guidance. They expect you to engage in consultative selling. This means they want both your creative suggestions and your assistance in helping them make decisions.

Power Phrases

Joint selling interviews with experienced agents, sales clinics, MDRT and association meetings will make it possible for you to build your inventory of phrases that move and motivate. Make them accessible by putting them in writing. Jot them down on three-by-five-inch index cards. Review them regularly and they will become a part of your selling style.

To get you started, you'll want to consider these:

No Need

- Life insurance is really nothing but money. You don't need more life insurance, but you do need more money. If you live, we call it thrift; when you die, we call it life insurance.

- Intelligent people buy life insurance—when they don't need it.

- You say, "I don't need it." With all respect, I ask you, "Could you change the 'I' to 'we' and still make that statement?"

- You'd give your life for Mary and Bill—why not insure it for them?

- No need, true; if you needed it, you couldn't get it.

No Money

- Don't be afraid to pay yourself first.

- No money—you don't want this to be permanent, do you?

- Earning money is easy—managing it successfully is hard. Life insurance makes its owner a successful manager of money.

- It's best to save first and spend last. There's no better time to begin that strategy than now.

No Hurry	• Every seventeen minutes someone buys life insurance who will not live to pay the second premium.
	• The only time people buy life insurance is when they *think* they need it. When they *know* they need it, they can't buy it.
	• I never met a person who planned to fail. I have met many people who have just failed to plan. Why not start planning now?
Inflation	• A widow doesn't ask what kind of dollars—just how many.
	• Inflation is the reason you should have purchased this last year.
	• Inflation of prices means inflation of income. Increased income into insurance will keep pace with inflation.
	• Life insurance is inflation proof.
	• Life insurance is inflation reactive.
	• I don't have to read the *Wall Street Journal* each morning to learn what happened to my cash values yesterday—I know they went up.
Wants Term, but Needs Permanent	• Will Rogers said, "I'm not so much interested in the return on my money as I am on the return of my money." You can't solve a permanent problem with temporary insurance.

- Buying and owning your home makes sense. It's better than renting. The same is true of life insurance.

- Term insurance is rented insurance and, therefore, the most expensive kind.

Disability Income

- Consider this: The chances of the average policyholder having a homeowner's claim within a year come to only one in twelve hundred. There's one chance in two hundred and fifty of an auto claim—and the odds are one hundred and fifty to one against the policyholder dying. *But, there's one chance in thirty that he or she will suffer a long-term disability.* That statistic speaks for itself . . . why not let it speak for you?

Business Insurance

- Do you own the business, or does the business own you?

- If a key employee isn't worth insuring, that person isn't a key employee.

Motivational Stories

As stated earlier, carefully selected stories, examples, and illustrations can exert tremendous power over your prospect's mind. There are only two kinds to select and use: *Those that you tell well and those that will be received well.*

The things that have happened to you, or around you, can be especially effective. Terry Bero, Equitable's fine producer in Green Bay, uses this one:

On May 7, 1975, I received a call at six-fifteen A.M. The wife of a very good friend of mine was calling to tell me that my friend had just died of cancer. My friend was fifty-one at the time of his death. He never finished high school. Nor did he ever work anywhere other than a factory where the maximum wage he earned was less than four dollars an hour.

But he had something much more valuable . . . he had friends wherever he went. A host of them. Why? Because he was a giver. He was a good listener. It's just too bad that he was a procrastinator, because he had never bought any life insurance. All he had was the two thousand dollars that was part of a group health package through his employer. His wife did get some death benefits: she received a free headstone from the Veteran's Administration for her late husband's eleven years of service in the marines. She also received two hundred and fifty dollars a month in Social Security.

Two years before my friend died, though, his wife had had a radical mastectomy due to cancer in the lymph nodes of her breast. Then, in October of 1981, she had a recurrence in her other breast and had a second mastectomy. No life insurance was in effect on her life, and now, obviously, none could be obtained.

One year after my friend died, his wife called me again to tell me that her youngest son, who was nineteen years old, had cancer. It was a mild type of skin cancer that is controllable. He also had no life insurance, and now, again, none could be obtained.

I don't know why these people never bought life insurance. I suspect that maybe the agents who approached them may have felt sympathy for them because of their low income. Maybe they couldn't break through the natural buyer-seller feud or the fear, or could not get them to see or correct their misunderstanding. Maybe it wasn't an agent's fault at all—it could be that the buyer-seller feud was too intense.

Whenever I'm with this woman today—whenever she accepts a check to help pay the mortgage or heating bill, or to pay the debts from medical expenses, she goes through a great deal of torment. I know, because the lady I speak of is my mother.

Irving Blackman, LL.B., CPA, and author of *Winning the Tax Game* shared this illustration at an MDRT meeting:

Do you know how to make a grown man cry? Tell him his business has been destroyed by fire, flood, or an act of God. A tragedy, but at least the loss was insured. What is even more important, Mr. Entrepreneur is there on the scene to assess the damage, to make plans, and to start rebuilding. Chances are he will make the business bigger and better than before. That is scene number one. Here is scene number two:

Even the most successful, egotistical, and immortal entrepreneur knows that some day he must go to the big business in the sky. That will not make him cry. He is too realistic for that. But tell him that after he is gone, his present plan—or better yet, his lack of plan— means the IRS will dismantle his business.

Imagine, if you will, our departed Mr. Entrepreneur in heaven, sitting on a cloud and talking to a representative of the IRS.

"Why?" he asks.
"To pay the federal estate-tax liability," answers the IRS representative.
"How?" he asks.
"By selling off the assets necessary to pay the tax."
"When?" he asks.
"Usually within two years after you are gone."
"By what right?" he asks.
"Federal Law."
"How much?" he asks.
"That depends on the value of your business."
"Good," says Mr. Entrepreneur. "I can show you just how little that business is worth without me."

"Sorry," responds the IRS representative. "It is too late for that now."

And that sets the stage for our mission as professionals to help the owner of the closely held corporation.

Naturally, your prospect listens to and becomes involved in stories like these. Your prospect likens the situation to his or her own. *Telling stories can be one of your most useful selling techniques.* But, remember, there are only two kinds to select and use; those you tell well and those that will be received well.

Frequently Encountered Objections and How to Handle Them

- Deciding on The Amount

The life-insurance purchase is much like the story told of the Arabian horseman. Riding by night, he heard a voice of authority commanding him to dismount and pick up pebbles. "In the morning you will be both glad and sad," the voice said.

At daybreak, the horseman awakened to discover that the pebbles he picked up were precious stones. Immediately, he was reminded of what the voice had predicted.

He was glad that he had gathered some, but, sad he hadn't gathered more.

- Asking the Wife, "What Do You think?"

Mary, before you respond, let me say this. Most wives I talk to think their husbands own enough insurance. Mary, I have yet to talk to the first widow who thought her husband owned enough.

Mary, in answering the question, "What do you think?" let me ask you, do you think this would be enough to take care of you and the children if something happens to Tom?

- Think It Over

I want to make certain I understand how you feel. You feel you need more insurance and you can afford it. It's just that you want to think it over. Is that right? In addition to that, is there any other reason why you wouldn't want to buy this plan this afternoon?

I think that's smart. You should never buy a plan this important without thinking it over. I wouldn't want you to ever buy anything that wasn't right for you. So, why don't we think this thing over together. Now, what questions do you have that we should think about?

- No Need

The life-insurance purchase is much like buying a parachute. You don't buy a parachute when you need it. You buy one when you don't need it. You make the intelligent decision to buy the parachute when you don't need it, so you'll have it when you do need it. If you need it and you don't have it—you can't get it! It's the same with life insurance. This makes sense, doesn't it?

- Compare

I want to make certain I understand how you feel. You like the plan, you feel you need more insurance, and you can afford it. It's just that you would like to compare, is that right? In addition to that, is there any other reason why you wouldn't want to buy this plan this afternoon?

I think that's smart. You should never buy a plan this important without comparing. But you know what would make me feel bad: if, while you were comparing, something happened that subsequently prevented you from qualifying for this preferred rate, or—perhaps—any rate. Or, if while you were comparing, something would happen to you. Let's move forward on this basis. You give me a check and I'll put your plan in effect today. Then, you go ahead and compare. In fact, I would compare with two or three companies. If you find a plan as good as this plan and an agent who will take care of you like I will, then go ahead and buy it and I'll give you your money back.

That's fair enough, isn't it?

- I'm Not Certain About Making A Financial Commitment Now

(Name), let's assume you are going to drive from Dallas (or wherever) to Denver. You wouldn't wait until all the traffic signals were green before you took off. You'd start when you saw the first Go signal. It's the same way with an individual starting on a program like this. If you wait until you can see all the way to age sixty-five, you will never have a program of any sort. But, (name), in almost every instance, when a person is doing the right thing and starts out, the lights work in his or her favor. Is there any better time for you to get started on this plan?

- A Red-letter Day Every Day

(Name), a few years ago, in a box on page one of the Baltimore Sun, *there appeared, about Christmastime, an article by a columnist who had visited an orphanage on the outskirts of the city to get material for a story.*

He went there with the idea of asking the children what they wanted for Christmas. He got the usual answers one would expect from small children, such as a teddy bear, tricycle, dolls, or a drum. One little girl told him she wanted a calendar with all red numbers on it. He asked her why, and she told him to come back to the dorm with her.

There, this youngster showed him a calendar over her bed on which all of the days, one at a time, up to the day he was there, were crossed off. He asked her why she did that and this little girl replied, "My mother can only come to visit me on the days that are red."

(Name), this plan would make every day a red-letter day for your children. This is what you want isn't it?

- Too Many Obligations

(Name), I understand what you mean. Have you ever thought of it this way? Suppose you and your family decide to go to the theater.

As you are taking your seats, you see your family doctor, your dentist, and your car dealer, each of whom you owe money.

You are all enjoying the show until suddenly you smell smoke and seconds later someone yells, "Fire!" So what do you do? You dash down to where the car dealer is and get him and his wife out to safety, while your family remains in danger. Then you rush back into the smoke and search out your doctor and dentist and lead them through the flames.

Then, if the roof hasn't caved in yet, you would go back to help your family! This isn't what you'd do, of course. Your greatest obligation is to those who are seated by your side. $ ＿＿ less a month to your creditors isn't going to put them in bankruptcy, but unless it is allocated to this plan, you may bankrupt your family. And you wouldn't want that, would you?

- Cautious About Making a Mistake

(Name), whether you buy this plan or not, you are going to make a mistake. If you buy it and don't need it—because you don't die or have plenty of income from some other source in later life—then you may have made a mistake. You have saved $ ＿＿ in premiums. We will give you back $ ＿＿ , which is a mistake that has earned you money. But maybe you could have earned more elsewhere, if you had conscientiously deposited the same amount on the same regular basis. To that extent only, it has been a mistake.

If you don't buy it, and your family needs it—then your mistake has cost them $ ＿＿ (face amount). Have you ever tried to wiggle out of a $ ＿＿ (face amount) mistake? Since the choice is yours, wouldn't you prefer a mistake that returns to you more than you put up, rather than a mistake that cost your family $ ＿＿ (face amount)?

132

Chapter Four Flashbacks

1. In making sales, the single most important factor is always
   your _____ *Confidence* _____ .
2. A planned presentation makes it possible for you to listen and
   study ____ *observe* ____ . You become a good "eye-listener."
3. The four essentials of an effective presentation are:
   a. It must ___ *Capture* ___ your prospect's instant and undi-
      vided ___ *attention* .
   b. It must ___ *arouse* ___interest by describing owner bene-
      fits and their ___ *advantages* ___to the prospect.
   c. It must ___ *create* ___desire by winning your prospect's
      ___ *confidence* ___ .
   d. It must ___ *motivate* ___your prospect to take ___ *action* ___
      now.
4. ___ *client understanding* ___ is the first secret of closing
   more and better sales.
5. A "controlled question" in selling is one where the response
   you'll receive is ___ *predictable* ___ .
6. An assertive attitude of ___ *expectancy* ___coupled with a planned
   ___ *strategy* ___leads to closing effectiveness.
7. Objections provide a clue to your prospect's ___ *thought* ___
   ___ *process* ___ Objections give you valuable feedback.
8. When objections surface, you handle them in one of three
   ways—you ___ *ignore* ___ , defer, or ___ *answer* ___them.
9. There are three basic reasons why a prospect is not sold on your
   recommendation:
   a. Something is not ___ *understood* ___
   b. Something is not ___ *believed* ___
   c. Something is being ___ *covered up* ___
10. Consultative selling requires you to make ___ *creative* ___sug-
    gestions and to ___ *assist* ___ the buyer in making a decision.

See page 233 for answers.

Self-Motivators for Making More and Better Sales

Nothing can hold back an idea whose time has come. You can give your prospect ownership of the idea of buying what you are trying to sell him by personalizing your recommendations. Remember that you will succeed in this only to the degree that you can speak the prospect's language.

Use a planned presentation and make your proposals distinctive. The following self-motivators will help you make more sales to quality prospects:

Hard planning makes easy selling.

The successful salesman pinches pennies for his prospect—he figures out how the premium can be paid.

Simplify your suggestions to gain understanding.

We learn, and sales are made, through the use of repetition . . . repetition . . . repetition.

You know your business, so speak as someone who has authority.

When a pause or interruption occurs, it's always wise to summarize.

The story method is the most effective means of making a prospect understand a point you wish to make or relate to a situation you are trying to describe. So build an inventory of stories and examples and practice telling them. Good storytellers are made, not born.

Your prospect has a free choice. You get your maximum share of the market's potential by creatively supplying what the prospect wants and needs.

—Walter H. Lowy

Commentary: The Art of Motivation

Nowhere in our formal educational systems is an individual taught how to motivate others or how to motivate himself at will. Yet the art of motivation is easy to teach and easy to learn.

Motivation is that which induces action or determines choice. It is that which provides a motive. A motive is the "inner urge" only within the individual that incites him to action, such as an instinct, emotion, habit, impulse, desire, or idea. It is the hope or other force that starts the individual in an attempt to produce specific results.

In the twentieth century, America has been particularly fortunate in developing a group of authors who have had, and do have, the unique talent to write in a manner that sows seeds of thought that motivate those who are searching for self-improvement to find it.

Defining a Positive Mental Attitude

These books do more than tell you how to motivate yourself and others at will with a Positive Mental Attitude—they motivate you to try to take immediate desirable action. But what is a Positive Mental Attitude?

A Positive Mental Attitude (PMA) for Americans is the right mental attitude under American concepts of the Judeo-Christian ethical and moral standards. It is most often comprised of the plus characteristics symbolized by such words as: optimism, hope, faith, honesty, integrity, altruism, generosity, kindliness, tolerance, tact, initiative, ambition, courage, self-discipline, and such expressions as the "golden rule"; respect for the life, property, and rights of others; and the dignity of labor. A Negative Mental Attitude (NMA) symbolizes opposite characteristics.

How I Discovered *Think and Grow Rich*

Napoleon Hill's book *Think and Grow Rich* was given to me by Morris Pickus—a nationally known sales executive—in 1937, toward the end of the Great Depression. I was ready. For, as a sales manager, I was searching for the secrets of success in motivating my representatives to become supersalesmen. Because I was searching, I recognized that which would help me. I got into action!

I sent a copy of *Think and Grow Rich* to each of my representatives. They, too, were ready. And many did . . . think and grow rich. Our national sales results were so phenomenal that I then recognized that exposing an ordinary sales representative to a modern inspirational self-help action book can make that individual a supersalesperson.

Throughout the years, I have raised men of humble means to great heights. For I found that the making of a sales rep begins with a modern inspirational self-help action book like this one.

Follow the Law of Success

To be a successful salesperson, you need to know and follow the Law of Success. And to be a successful person, you must understand the Law of Success well enough to know that principles that work in one phase of your life will work in other phases of the series of experiences that comprise your life—personal, family, social, or business. One very simple analogy: speed laws apply whether you are operating an automobile, a truck, or a motorcycle. So it is with the Law of Success; to know the richness of a successful life, the guidelines, principles, and disciplines apply in dealings with your family and friends as well as with colleagues, subordinates, business associates, or clients.

To achieve success, you have developed the habit, through association of ideas, of consistently applying universal principles, right? Why not give yourself a test with regard to the following components of the Law of Success. Do you understand and apply them in all phases in your life?

- *You are the most important living person as far as you and your life are concerned.* For you can direct your thoughts, control your emotions, and ordain your destiny—if you know how to, and if you set high goals and daily strive to achieve them.
- *The whole is equal to the sum of all its parts.* This applies to every phase of your life—personal, family, social, and business. Therefore, if you will analyze the principles that help you achieve any worthy success, they can be applied to achieve success in every phase of your living experience.
- *In* Success through a Positive Mental Attitude, *by Napoleon Hill and me, we refer to seventeen Principles of Success:*
  1. A Positive Mental Attitude
  2. Definiteness of purpose
  3. Going the extra mile
  4. Accurate thinking
  5. Self-discipline
  6. The mastermind
  7. Applied faith
  8. A pleasing personality
  9. Personal initiative
  10. Enthusiasm
  11. Controlled attention
  12. Teamwork
  13. Learning from defeat
  14. Creative vision
  15. Budgeting time and money
  16. Maintaining sound physical and mental health
  17. Using cosmic habit force (universal law)

Even though you've read these, it is most helpful to review them and deliberately try to understand, comprehend, digest, and apply the principles, rather than merely memorize facts or formulas.

- *To be truly successful, prove your sincerity—practice what you preach.*

- *Use PMA to keep your mind on what you want and off of what you don't want.* This is the secret in solving problems instead of worrying about them.
- *You know the golden rule: Do unto others as you would have them do unto you.* Do you actually try to live up to the golden rule instead of merely knowing the words? Do you consciously avoid doing to others what you don't want them to do to you?
- Your greatest power is the power of prayer—if you know how to pray with PMA and follow through with action.

In the Lord's Prayer, there is a request: ". . . forgive us our debts as we forgive our debtors . . ." or ". . . forgive us our trespasses as we forgive those who trespass against us . . ." If you repeat the Lord's Prayer, do you think about what you are asking? In your daily life, how readily do you forgive?

- You don't always get in life what you expect—unless you inspect with regularity. Example: When you give instructions, do you assume your instructions were understood, or do you ask questions to see if you've made yourself clear?
- PMA action is imperative for success in any worthy human activity.

"Think like a man of action and act like a man of thought."

—Henri Bergson

"Sow a thought, and you reap an act; sow an act, and you reap a habit; sow a habit, and you reap a character; sow a character, and you reap a destiny."

—G. D. Boardman

You establish a habit of thought or action by repetition, repetition, repetition. You can eliminate an undesirable habit by setting a specific goal for the right habit—if you write it down and review it daily during your thinking, planning, and study time—provided that you follow through with the desired action.

138

"The world's great men have not commonly been great scholars, nor its great scholars great men."

— Oliver Wendell Holmes

What do the above principles mean to you? Think about them, then decide what action you will take in applying them.

What New Year's resolutions did you make for this year? Did you actually achieve them? What New Year's resolutions will you make for next year? If you do make resolutions for the coming year, you can assure their achievement by writing them down and inspecting your progress daily with PMA—but you follow through with ACTION!

Will you? It's up to you. Is it worth the effort? You decide!

—*W. Clement Stone*

Chapter Five

The Power of
Professionalism

Building A Professional Image

Although products change, the people purchasing those products don't change. Prospects may talk today about cash flow instead of earnings. They may be more knowledgeable about life insurance today. But it takes an agent to motivate them to buy. Last year, ninety-five percent of the life insurance purchased was purchased through the good work of an agent.

— D. E. Laughlin, CLU

Companies rarely have a product design or premium advantage for very long. Their competitive edge, their only major advantage, lies in the professional manner in which their agents deliver distinctive service. Your image in business circles and your community has a *direct bearing* on your sales performance. In this chapter, we will examine specific ways you can build your image as a professional.

Image-building and professionalism are closely linked to the tasks of keeping business on the books and gaining introductions to referrals. We begin by studying these two final steps in the sales process.

Your Stock-In-Trade

Professionalism in selling insurance and equity products requires prompt, personal follow-through. As Dr. Mike Mescon, dean of the Business School at Georgia State, says: "Good or bad, right or wrong, clients are most likely to recall the last—not the first—experience. They remember the end of the story, not the beginning. Clients want consistent service from start to finish." As a professional, you want to deliver consistent service and achieve client satisfaction.

Strive to make client satisfaction your "stock-in-trade." How do you do this? Quite simply. Make certain your prospects get more in the way of service from you than they expect. Make certain they get more than they pay for. And make certain they get more in the way of client service and information from you than they can possibly get from your competitors.

"Spoil your clients," says Connecticut Mutual's Calvin Hunt. "Give them more and better service than they thought was possible. Everybody gets an annual review from me, either by letter, telephone, or in person. I send birthday cards with personal notes in them, and Christmas cards. I want clients to know I appreciate their business and confidence. Repeat business comes easy when you go out of your way to spoil them."

Establishing A Client

You've secured the signed app. You have picked up the initial premium. Your prospect's application has gone to the home office. The contract soon returns to you for delivery. *Remember, the person who purchased the policy and paid the premium did so because he or she had confidence in you and the service you would provide.* Whether or not that confidence is maintained and enhanced depends on you and the manner in which you handle this first "sale after the sale"—sale no. 5, Establishing A Client.

It takes less effort to keep an existing client satisfied than to get a new prospect interested. Studies show that in nearly sixty percent of all life insurance lapses, the policy terminates with the second premium. These same studies conclude that after your client pays four premiums, lapses reduce dramatically. Obviously, if you proceed on the basis that your job has been completed when you process the application with the initial premium, you're deceiving yourself.

The income you build from improved client retention alone makes planned service calls a sound business practice. Retaining clients depends on keeping promises—the promises of future services you made or at least implied early in the selling process.

Your ability as a sales professional will be judged more by the number of clients you retain than by the amount of new business you develop. Here are proven techniques to help improve the retention rate of your business:

- *Seek quality prospects.* Work with individuals who have the ability and character to buy and keep what they buy. You want repeat buyers.
- *Get a substantial amount of cash with the application.* This solidifies the sale, avoiding the need for additional selling at policy-delivery time.
- *Suit the size of the premium and the premium frequency to your prospect.* It might be ideal if you could get nothing but annual premiums. This is, of course, a practical impossibility because selling some people on an annual basis may result in difficulty for them in meeting the next premium when due. The monthly, preauthorized-check payment plan has proved to be the most popular method for most buyers. It also has a good record for retention.
- *Sell on the basis of needs.* When a policy covers a specific need—and the client understands that it does—there is less likelihood the owner will let it go without a struggle to keep it.
- *Resell and explain the benefits of the policy upon delivery.* Between the time a new client signs an application and the receipt of the policy, enthusiasm for the purchase may cool considerably. Take time to explain how valuable the purchase is and what its specific place is in the client's overall program.
- *Try for a larger average sale.* Larger sales are directly related to income, and the amount of discretionary income a client has is linked to retention.
- *Sell temporary forms of protection only when they are absolutely needed.* The lapse rate on term insurance is generally high, and

term policies are vulnerable to conversion and replacement by other agents. Schedule the conversion of the term insurance you sell.

- *Follow up second premiums.* Make it a point to call back on new clients about the time their second premium is due. You'll need a reason for doing so — you don't want clients to think you are prying or checking up on them. One method of opening the way for follow-up calls, after you've written the "thank you" letter discussed in the next section, is to make a practice of sending new clients newspaper clippings that you think might interest them. A call to ask if they got a particular clipping provides an opening to inquire about the new contract or to point out additional features. Do everything you can to help get the second and subsequent premiums paid.
- *Keep in touch with all of your clients.* Make a contact with every client at least once a year. It is logical to do this on birthdays, or when you know the client may have increased needs.
- *Develop the service point of view.* Dedicate yourself to achieving the reputation of being an agent who is responsive to clients' needs and organized for delivering prompt, accurate, courteous follow-up service.

Making the Sale Solid

Assure your new client that he or she has made an intelligent decision. An effective way to do this is to write a congratulatory letter. This adds a distinctive touch. It displays professionalism. Many of your competitors will not be as well organized or take the time to write.

We suggest you write a letter after every sale and that you mail it as soon after the sale as possible. The letter shown in Figure 5-1, written by our associate, Gary Newell, is of the type used by a number of successful agents.

You may wish to add a postscript to assure your client that all the necessary papers have been processed and to remind him or her of your scheduled appointment to deliver the policy in person.

In-Person Delivery

When you receive the contract, deliver it promptly and in person. You are now meeting with someone who has been converted from a prospect to a buyer. *Delivery sets the stage to make this buyer a client.* And as David Hilton at Northwestern Mutual in Chicago says: "It's the number of clients we have that determines our income."

You may motivate the prospect to buy. You may gain his or her confidence, but maintaining that confidence is an additional responsibility. *Building client confidence begins with the delivery of the contract.* This "eyeball-to-eyeball" interview with your new client permits you to accomplish five important objectives:

1. To resell the need and make the sale solid
2. To remind your client of the next premium date
3. To set the stage for future purchases
4. To build an ongoing relationship with your client
5. To get referred-lead introductions.

Making the "Delivery Interview"

A favorable delivery permits you to resell yourself as a professional. Prepare to make it a great occasion.

Have a policy summary neatly prepared and bound. Make it a standard procedure to enclose the policy in an attractive policy wallet with the prospect's name embossed. It will make an even better impression if you have the names of family members embossed as well.

Your clients recognize professionalism when they see it and they associate it with dependability. An organized, professional procedure for the delivery of the policy includes these points:

- *Congratulate Your Client*—Commend the buyer for having the wisdom to plan for the future.
- *Resell the Need*—Get your client to agree again on the objectives he or she has set, personal or otherwise. Then show how the purchase of insurance attains these objectives. *Every buyer wants to be reassured that he or she has done the right thing.*

Figure 5-1

GARY W. NEWELL
INSURANCE BROKER

Business	17110 DALLAS PARKWAY	Home
(214) 380-1362	SUITE 260	(214) 233-8808
	DALLAS, TEXAS 75248	

Mr. Robert Scoddler
1516 Woodward Avenue
Dallas, Texas 75240

Dear Bob:

I want to thank you and let you know how much I appreciate
your business. As the years roll on, Bob, I assure you I'll
strive to merit your confidence.

Since changes in family and financial conditions make it desirable to review your program periodically, I'll keep in touch
wih you and call on you from time to time. As we've discussed, it's important for us to review your financial plan in
depth at least once a year.

Naturally, I'll consider it a privilege to be consulted by you or
your friends whenever there are questions regarding financial matters. Bob, I'd like very much to have you consider me
your financial adviser. Please feel free to call any time you
have questions about insurance taxes, pension benefits, or
tax shelters.

I am looking forward to seeing you soon.

Yours sincerely,

Gary Newell

GN/laf

- *Review the "Owner Benefits"*—Explain what happens if the buyer lives—or dies—or needs funds.
- *Prepare for the Next Sale*—Point out any needs and objectives that are not yet covered. Get a commitment on what needs your client feels should be handled next.
- *Schedule the Next Interview*—Decide upon the date for your next visit.
- *Develop Referred-Lead Introductions*—Expect your new client to give you introductions to your new prospects.

Remember, seeing clients on a regular basis creates opportunities to sell as well as to provide service.

Completing the Sales Process

We once saw an interesting survey of 4,165 buyers of life insurance. It showed that two out of three had never been asked for referrals. Even more revealing was the fact that over ninety percent of those interviewed indicated they would have given referrals, had they been asked. The reason for their willingness to do so is elementary: people like helping others; they like influencing the success of those they respect. Moreover, when a third party buys, it supports their own earlier decision to buy. They like their decisions to be reinforced by others.

The conclusion is inescapable: sales generate more sales, if you let them. This brings us to sale no. 6—Getting Referred Lead Endorsements. Ask yourself these questions: *"Who can I get in front of and possibly sell a bit easier now because I made this sale?" "Who will give me a favorable interview simply because this client recommends me?"*

Help is Given to Those Who Ask

The strategy we recommend was developed by Bob Reece, an outstanding Equitable agent in Los Angeles. Bob uses this effective approach for developing referred leads:

I would like very much to ask you to help me. We study our business closely and our surveys reveal to us that as much as seventy percent

Exhibit 5-1 — The Anatomy of a Satisfied Client

One of the most creative agents we've ever been associated with is Equitable's Hall of Famer, Bill Mansfield. Each year Bill, a life member of the MDRT, generates most of his business from servicing existing clients.

This exhibit shows you an actual example of Bill's commissions from a single client — the kind of success that can be yours, too.

First-Year Commissions

$ 252.00	On July 14, 1959, a $10,000 Whole Life Policy was sold to the treasurer of a company to assist him in covering a new mortgage. On January 9, 1960, the company purchased $400,000 of Whole Life on the president with a $300,000 Term rider owned by the president's wife. On January 1, 1961, the company purchased a group hospital and medical plan for the thirty-two salaried employees. On September 1, 1961, Group Life was added to the plan.
11,138.00	
2,560.00	
980.00	
4,245.00	On December 28, 1962, the wife of the president converted $200,000 of the Term rider to Whole Life.
1,174.00	On June 26, 1963, the treasurer purchased a $100,000 Whole Life on a Split-Dollar plan.
5,354.00	On May 5, 1964, the president sold the company to his two vice-presidents and the company purchased $75,000 Whole Life and $300,000 Term on each new owner. They each also purchased $100,000 of Whole Life on a Split-Dollar basis.
1,680.00	
4,466.00	
2,350.00	On September 9, 1964, a $100,000 Split-Dollar policy was written on the plant manager of the original company.
13,588.00	On May 17, 1965, the company converted the $300,000 of Term on each stockholder to Whole Life. On May 17, 1967, the company purchased $125,000 Whole Life on each stockholder to bring the stock retirement coverage to $500,000.
6,193.00	
5,076.00	In September 1967, the three officers took medical examinations to raise their Group Life to $100,000. On the basis of the medical information, $100,000 of Whole Life was ordered and placed on the two stockholders.
2,750.00	On October 1, 1967, a group pension plan was adapted covering the salaried employees.
5,710.00	On January 14, 1970, the company purchased $100,000 Whole Life on each stockholder.
39,414.00	On October 4, 1973, the company purchased $500,000 Whole Life on each of the stockholders to bring the coverage on each to $1,100,000, including a "D" rating on one of the stockholders.

Exhibit 5-1 Continued

6,190.00   On June 1, 1973, the hourly employees were covered under a Group Life and Hospital Medical Plan

In the meantime, the former president purchased a nursing home and purchased $200,000 Whole Life on the man hired to operate the home. On April
2,470.00   2, 1968, the nursing home administrator purchased $100,000 Whole Life
2,780.00   and $500,000 Term on his own life. On January 21, 1973, the administrator converted $300,000 of the Term to Whole Life and on April 4, 1975,
3,190.00   the administrator purchased another $100,000 of Term to cover a
215.00   bank loan.

In the meantime, the new president referred me to his son, who was in business with three other men. They elected to cover a stock retirement plan.
5,387.00   Their company purchased $100,000 Whole Life on each of the four stock-
11,161.00   holders. A year later, $200,000 of Whole Life was placed on each of the
245.00   stockholders. Later, one of the four purchased a $53,000 Mortgage Term contract.

In 1982, four Split-Dollar Whole Life contracts were purchased on each of
6,545.00   these stockholders.

One of the original stockholders retired and was replaced by a new stock-
3,064.00   holder and the company purchased $50,000 of Whole Life and $100,000 Split-Dollar Whole Life rated "E".

Another one of these stockholders purchased $200,000 of Term to cover a
192.00   divorce settlement.

6,350.00   Disability insurance was then placed on the four stockholders.

34,070.00   On May 18, 1982, $1,000,000 of additional stock retirement coverage on the president of the original company.

On May 30, 1985, the treasurer attempted to murder the president and after wounding him, committed suicide. He was replaced by a new treasurer and
10,604.00   the company purchased $500,000 Whole Life on the new treasurer and $500,000 on a new vice-president on Split-Dollar basis.

1,600.00   A former vice-president who had retired, purchased $41,700 Whole Life to cover the collateral-assignment loan of his Split-Dollar policy.

7,614.00   The president purchased $200,000 of a new Split-Dollar coverage.

5,560.00   A new company subsidiary was established and $250,000 Whole Life was
1,100.00   placed on the president of the subsidiary, and $500,000 of Term on a plant manager

$ 217,267.00   Total – First-Year Commissions
350,000.00   Renewal and Service Fees

$ 567,267.00   Total

of our new business comes to us from satisfied clients like you and those you recommend. I would like to have you help me by giving some thought now to someone you know who appears to have a need for insurance, and who would be receptive to me and the procedure I've used in handling your insurance and financial affairs.

This is a strategy for you to master and perfect. When using it, poise your pen to write the client's response on a prospect card. This communicates to the client that you fully expect him or her to give you some names.

Remember, an introduction carries with it the element of being an endorsement.

Another effective strategy for obtaining referred leads comes from paying attention during the interviews you have with your prospect. After the prospect becomes a client, use a casual, conversational tone to bring up names that he or she might give you. In other words, you might say something like:

(Name), the last time I was here you mentioned that Tom Adams was a friend you have golfed with for several years. I'm wondering if the Adamses are the type of people that might be interested in the kind of work we do.

Another effective way to develop referred-lead introductions is:

(Name), who are the three top people in your company I can approach about the work we do? (no pause) When I call for an appointment, I will say—I asked (name) who were the three top people in his company I could contact about the work I do at (company). (Name) gave me your name and told me about the fine job you do. . . . (Name), I'll not always get an appointment—but the person you refer will always appreciate your recognition of his or her performance.

A Stationery Gift Gambit—Discipline yourself to get introductions and information. Practice to develop this skill in developing referrals. Remember, getting one introduction to a referral you will approach, develop, and sell is much better than a list of names that don't spark your enthusiasm to make the initial call. Like most substantial producers, Barbara Cornelius, Equitable of Iowa's sales manager in Detroit, wants her reputation to precede her. Barbara develops referred-lead endorsements using a most unusual strategy.

First Barbara asks each client to choose a print style that appeals to them from a layout sheet. When she returns to deliver the contract, Barbara presents her client with an attractive gift of personalized stationery. She shows the client a letter of introduction (see Figure 5-2). Barbara then asks if she can prepare this same letter on the new stationery, for the client's signature to be mailed to twenty referrals. She says she receives a positive response from most clients.

Calling your shots—The late Ed O'Shaugnessy employed a little different twist to getting an endorsement. He used this idea to lead his company in sales: after the policy had been explained and delivered to the client, instead of asking for names, Ed would say:

> *I intend to call on Jim Smith in your company. If he has any questions about the work I do, would you mind my using your name and referring him to you?*

This produces excellent results. It's especially good to use after you have sold insurance to a key person who can be influential with other associates or subordinates.

In the course of discussion with your client ask about the possible response you might expect from the referred prospects. Also, ascertain common interests or affiliations you might have with the referrals that could be helpful to you in quickly developing a good relationship with them. *Thank your client and let the client know you will keep him or her informed of your results.* Be certain to report back—every time! It will do much to strengthen your client relationship.

Getting referred leads makes each sale more productive and keeps you on "the selling track." It maintains momentum because you always have qualified prospects to see—lots of them.

Remember, the better the agent, the higher the percentage of his or her business that is derived from satisfied clients.

Figure 5-2

January 15, 1987

Mr. and Mrs. Ronald Rollins
6042 Campbell Drive
Royal Oak, Michigan

Dear Ron and Linda:

In these days of tax reform, changing interest rates, and varying economic conditions, we have determined that financial management is an important consideration for us. In realizing this, we have consulted Barbara Cornelius of the financial planning firm, P. Terry Knight and Associates.

They specialize in helping individuals prepare and then implement plans for personal estate accumulation, preservation, and distribution. With her help, we have been able to recognize several ways to maximize our current disposable income and organize our assets to meet our short- and long-term objectives.

Because Barbara has been of great help to us, we have asked her to call you. We are confident that any time you might spend with her will be a worthwhile investment.

Sincerely,

Lisa and David Barner

Increasing Your Effectiveness

As a general rule, agents are underpaid for the amount of sales effort put in during the first five years. After these apprenticeship years, they tend to be overpaid. There are several reasons for this. Selling skills take time to develop, and knowledge and confidence grow along with those skills. The experienced agent is better disciplined and, obviously, has a more extensive referral network. Studies have shown that only fifteen percent of your success will be determined by technical knowledge. This means that eighty-five percent of your effectiveness is determined by your ability to manage yourself and your skills in meeting and dealing with prospects.

Increasing Your "Professional Equity"

Jim Cathcart, author of *The Business of Selling*, refers to "professional equity" as the degree of ownership you acquire in your career. This might be considered your professional net worth, according to Jim. The assets that make up your "equity" as an agent include your relationship-building skills, your credentials, your product knowledge, and your contacts.

Here are three ways to enhance your "professional equity":

1. *Build Relationships* — Many say it's not *what* you know, it's *who* you know. When it comes to prospective buyers, it's not *who* you know, it's *how* you know them. Having contacts in the upscale marketplace is desirable. However, you must have credibility with these prospects. They must like and respect you.

Relationship building is a skill that can and must be developed. It requires you to be mindful of things you can do or say to build confidence and establish trust. Examine each of these proven methods for building relationships:

- *Look for Communications Opportunities* — There are many reasons you can find to send business, prospects, or information to prospects and clients. Ask yourself this question regularly — "What can I do to help my prospect and client's business?"

153

- *Persuade Others to Assist You* — Get them to make introductions or give you endorsements. Remember, people are happy to help you when you ask them and show them how.
- *Make Prospects Feel Important* — Look for ways in which you can genuinely compliment them on their intelligence, appearance, achievements, or possessions.
- *Uncover Common Interests* — Asking prospects for their opinions will reveal areas of mutual interest, often unusual ones.
- *Join the Client-Admiration Society* — Make it a practice to acknowledge or admire significant details about members of their families. As Mark McCormick says: "If you have a client you want to impress, do something for his or her kids."
- *Be a Well-Wisher* — Deliver one birthday greeting every week — in person.

Practice these techniques until they become second nature. You will find that they can make relationships with clients bloom like the desert after a rainstorm.

2. *Acquire Symbols of Excellence* — The insurance industry prides itself on keeping standards high for the various awards it has developed. Earn the professional degrees and strive to achieve the awards identified with excellence. These credentials will cause you to become known in your marketplace, and will lubricate all future introductions.

Become a "ten-letter" agent as early in your career as possible. You do this by putting CLU, MDRT and NQA behind your name. In today's environment, adding ChFC, CPCU, CFP, and RHU will enhance your credibility, too. These degrees and awards identify agents who are competent, competitive, and consistent.

3. *Stay Contact-Conscious* — Nearly all high-performing agents are involved in their community. They are active members of church, civic cultural, and local business organizations. They tend to assume leadership roles, being communicators rather than passive observers. You take a lot out of the community you live in. People do business with you. You earn commissions. It stands to reason that you need to give something back. Don't disregard the nonprofessional community. Devote time

to organizations like the Kidney Foundation, American Red Cross, March of Dimes, or other similar groups.

The insurance business is a contact business. Breakfast and luncheon clubs offer a network of business and social contacts. They usually feature a program, sometimes with outside speakers. But they can also widen your contact base.

You also need to become involved with the professional community. The well-known financial consultant, Dr. Robert Oberst, speaking at the International Association of Financial Planners Conference, explained the value of his membership in the Red Bank, New Jersey, Estate Planning Council. Similar councils around the country are made up of trust officers, accountants, insurance agents, attorneys, and financial planners. Dr. Oberst said:

"By becoming involved in these types of organizations, you accomplish several things. One, you learn a great deal. Where else can you sit next to a skilled attorney and exchange ideas with him on estate matters? Furthermore, the professionals in the council will discover that you are interested. You want to learn. You have a good working knowledge of your own specialized profession.

"If you can contribute something meaningful, the accountants and attorneys will come to you for advice on matters where they know you are trained and skilled. Then they will begin referring clients to you."

Creating an Image

What kind of image do you want to develop in the minds of your prospects and clients? How do you want to be perceived? The National Association of Life Underwriters spends nearly two hundred fifty thousand dollars each year to build the public image of its members. The Institute of Life Insurance and insurance companies spend millions of dollars each year to build a favorable image of their products, services, and agents. It's up to you to reinforce these positive impressions in your personal relations. When your prospects, clients, and community leaders are surveyed, you want them to put you in the same category as any other professional—their doctor, accountant, banker, lawyer, or minister.

Building a professional image tends to soften your market. It facilitates the process of turning prospects into clients and of making additional sales to existing clients. Building a professional image brings growth to your business.

Here are eight ways in which you can build your professional image.

1. *Project Success*—Prospects focus on *you* before they focus on what you are selling. Their perception of you carries considerable influence in their decision to do business with you. The way you look and behave says things to prospects and clients. It tells them whether you are a seasoned professional or an amateur. Study successful agents. Observe the types of appearance and behavior they exhibit. Cultivate an appearance that projects an image of competence, confidence, and pride in your sales performance. *A good rule to follow is to always look as if you care how you look.*

2. *Project Professionalism*—When prospects and clients come into your office they expect to see professionalism. *Make certain they see and feel evidence of success.* They should be greeted warmly and made to feel welcome. In addition to attractive and appropriate artwork, they should see your professional designations on your office walls.

3. *Project Good Taste*—Carefully consider the design of business cards and stationery you use. Keep both conservative. Make sure the title you use reflects what you do. An attractive brochure can enhance your image. It can display your credentials and communicate to your prospects the broad range of products you sell.

4. *Project a Message*—Regular, informative mailings to key clients and prospects keep your name in circulation, in mind. It does this in an inexpensive, positive, nonthreatening way. You will want to investigate the several financial and insurance-related newsletters that can be sent monthly or quarterly.

Greg Wright, CFP with Mass Mutual in Indianapolis, says: "My marketing philosophy is that everyone I meet eventually will need to purchase an insurance or investment product that I sell. It may be today, next month, or next year. The problem is to maintain contact with these prospective customers. My solution was to develop a monthly newsletter.

This delivers meaningful financial data to my suspects, prospects, and customers every month. It contains short articles that are generic and fit on a one-page self-mailer. The newsletter contains my picture and a postage-paid reply card. The newsletter reminds people that I'm a financial planner and am in the business of selling insurance and investment products. When they have a financial concern or question, I'm a familiar face and name."

5. *Target Advertising* — When you advertise in professional journals and newsletters, you can build your image with certain target groups, such as attorneys, CPAs, and engineers. Advertising is expensive. The results are generally hard to measure. You'll want to use it only when the publication targets the audience you are trying to reach.

6. *Write Articles* — An excellent strategy to help you become known for what you know is to publish articles. Trade-association journals and newsletters are usually looking for articles. Published material establishes you as an authority. Circulating reprints will have a powerful influence on prospects and clients.

7. *Schedule Speaking Engagements* — Use industry, club, and community speaking engagements to build your image in front of potential clients. These organizations are generally looking for speakers on financial and investment topics. As with written articles, speeches create a powerful image of you as an authority.

8. *Conduct Seminars* — Seminar selling can be a most effective way to build your professional image. Seminars can be sponsored by other groups, or you can promote them on your own. Should you choose to co-operate with other groups in jointly sponsoring the seminar, the following are organizations you can consider:

- medical associations
- dental societies
- credit or retail associations
- political groups
- trade and civic groups
- church organizations
- foundations and charities
- nonprofit organizations
- colleges
- private schools

If you are prepared to make the commitment of time, effort, and money, you will find sponsoring your own seminars to be a profitable, image-building endeavor. There are two kinds of seminars you can give: educational and motivational. The purpose of an educational seminar is to educate your audience. A motivational seminar's aim is to motivate your audience into taking some action you want them to take. Oftentimes, seminars can be conducted in cooperation with other carefully selected professionals. Working with a well-known accountant or lawyer will do much to enhance your image and build your reputation.

The Common Thread

We once heard author Og Mandino tell a story that drives home the dominant theme of this chapter. It went like this:

We all need help to achieve, to grow, to recover from disaster. Back in the fifteenth century, in a little village right outside of Nuremberg, Germany, lived a family with fifteen children. Daddy worked three jobs—just to keep food on the table for this tribe. Two of the boys had an ambition, a dream. It was the same dream. They both wanted to go to the Art Academy in Nuremberg. But they knew full well that there was no way their daddy would ever be able to afford to send either one of them.

So these two brothers, with similar talents and interests, worked up a pact. They would toss a coin. The winner would go to the academy. The loser would go down into the mines, and with his pay, would support the winner's studies. Four years later, when the first one was graduated, he would go into the mines or use the income from his commissioned artwork to support his brother, who would attend the academy and obtain his art degree, too.

One morning they tossed the coin. Albrecht Dürer won. Albert Dürer lost. Albrecht went off to the academy, and Albert went down into the mines.

Albrecht was an immediate sensation at the academy. He was better than any of his professors. In his paintings, in his line drawings, in his engravings, in his woodcuts—he was just a natural. By his third year in school, Albrecht was earning enough in commissions to support himself. And when he graduated, the family held a large party out on the lawn. All the children were there. Albrecht, from the head of the table, arose with a glass of wine. He offered a toast to his beloved brother, for all that Albert had done for him. And he finished the toast by saying, ". . . and now, Albert—now it's your turn. You can go to the academy, and I will take care of you."

All eyes turned to the other end of the table. Albert was staring down at his hands and shaking his head saying, "No, no, no."

Finally Albert rose, tears streaming down his cheeks. He looked down at Albrecht and said, "Albrecht, dear brother, it's too late for me. Look what four years in the mines have done to my hands! I've broken every finger at least once. I have arthritis in my left hand so bad that I can't even hold a piece of bread. I can't even lift my hands together so that I could return your toast properly. No, brother, I love you, but it is too late, much too late for me."

Four hundred years have passed. Albrecht Dürer's artwork hangs in every great museum in the world. And yet, most know him for just one of his creations. Because one day, Albrecht Dürer honored his beloved brother by painting his hands.

Some of you have it hanging in your home. Or, maybe, you wear it around your neck as a charm. Maybe you have it in your office as bookends. But I know all of you know it. Because today we call it "The Praying Hands."

The next time you look at that marvelous piece of work—take a good look at it. Let it remind you of the common thread that runs through the life of every true success story in this business. If you could sit the great agents down in private and talk to them, if you could let them really open their hearts to you, every one of them would freely admit that they could not and that they did not make it alone. No agent—no agent, no matter how great—achieves outstanding success alone.

Like all the rest, you need help to achieve, to grow, and to develop the power of professionalism. You'll be surprised how close that help is, if you ask and expect it in the ways described in this chapter.

Chapter Five Flashbacks

1. Image-building and professionalism are closely allied with keeping business on the books and gaining _____ _____ .

2. Persistency of business improves when you
   a. look for _____prospects
   b. sell on the basis of _____
   c. follow up on the _____premiums
   d. develop the _____point of view.

3. Writing a congratulatory letter adds a _____ touch and displays _____ .

4. The in-person delivery of the contract accomplishes several things:
   a. _____the need
   b. _____of next premium
   c. sets the stage for _____ _____
   d. builds the _____
   e. gets _____.

5. An introduction to a referral carries with it the element of being an _____.

6. Sale no. 6, _____ , makes the sale productive and keeps you on "_____."

7. _____ of your effectiveness is determined by your ability to _____yourself and your skills in _____ and _____with prospects.

8. "Professional equity" is the degree of _____ you acquire in your career.

9. You enhance your professional equity in these ways:
   a. build _____

    b. acquire symbols of _____

    c. stay _____-conscious.

10. You create a professional image in these ways:

    a. project _____

    b. project professionalism at _____

    c. examine cards, _____and brochures

    d. organize _____

    e. write _____

    f. schedule _____

    g. conduct _____

    h. target _____

_____

See page 234 for answers.

Self-Motivators for Building a Professional Image

"He who steals my purse steals trash . . . but he that filches from me my good name . . . makes me poor indeed." William Shakespeare, the author of those words, had a keen understanding of the importance of appearances and reputation. He made high comedy and classic tragedy of these human characteristics, and the agent who understands them will set sales records.

A professional image, *your good name in the field,* is everything. Make the following self-motivators your own, and think of others that will help you create the kind of professional image you want.

Never make a sales call without getting approval from the man or woman in the mirror.

Client satisfaction is your stock-in-trade—don't leave a client without it.

Deliver contracts promptly and in person.

Good news in your client's life is good news for you—it's an opportunity to write a letter of congratulations. People remember praises.

Your next sale depends on your client's friends—so get referral introductions and information.

Make friends with your prospects and clients, then sell to your friends.

Acquire symbols of excellence.

Stay contact-conscious.

Project success and professionalism in everything you do.

Effective selling involves not only the powers of persuasion, the art of negotiation, persistence and timing—it also demands, as much as any of these, the proper marketability of your product.

—Mark McCormack

Commentary:
Cultivate a 'Divine
Discontent'

"Develop inspirational dissatisfaction! I would urge that you be dissatis-fied. Not dissatisfied in the sense of disgruntlement, but dissatisfied in the sense of that 'divine discontent' that throughout the history of the world has produced all real progress and reform. I hope that you will never be satisfied. I hope you will constantly feel the urge to improve and perfect not only yourself but the world around you."

That quote from Charles Becker, then president of Franklin Life In-surance Company, was used by Dr. Napoleon Hill and me in *Success Through a Positive Mental Attitude*. It is as appropriate now as it was in 1960 — perhaps more so.

I evaluate my writings, speeches, and teachings by one standard only: *Results* — specifically, what positive *action* my readers or listening audi-ence actually takes because of my efforts.

Because you don't always get what you expect unless you inspect, it pays to ask yourself a question and take the thinking time to come up with the answer that will motivate you to *action*. If I were you, the reader, I would immediately ask myself, "What is the principle in Charles Becker's comments? What does it mean to me? What *action* will I take that I would not have, had I not read the quotation?"

As you check your progress toward your goals each day, be discon-tented in the sense of not being happy with things as they are, but be happy in the thought you have within you, be happy in the power you possess to change yourself and things for the better. That's the kind of discontent author Ben Sweetland had in mind when he wrote:

> *Every invention listed in the United States Patent Office is the result of discontent. The inventor, not being satisfied with something as it was, found a way to improve it.*
>
> *If people were satisfied with horse-and-buggy transportation, we would not have automobiles, trains, and planes.*
>
> *If people were satisfied with ordinary postal communication, we would not have the telephone.*
>
> *Every improvement of any kind reflects discontent with things as they were.*
>
> *And no man attempts to improve himself mentally or physically as long as he is contented with himself as he is.*

Because at school you were not taught how to recognize, relate, assimilate, and apply principles into your own life from what you read, see, hear and experience, especially from other disciplines, you may now be momentarily inspired yet do nothing to develop for yourself true Inspirational Dissatisfaction.

But it's not too late to begin. You can start now! You can pay the price that costs you nothing in dollars and cents. You can do what great achievers have developed the *habit* of doing. You can start by setting aside a half hour the day you read this commentary and set a very high goal that benefits both yourself and others.

If you take a half hour of thinking-time today and repeat the practice daily, you will develop the *habit* of a half hour of thinking-time daily toward achieving your Big Goal that may seem impossible to others. A *habit* is established by repetition . . . repetition . . . repetition.

Evaluate your reaction to what you have just read by what ACTION you do or do not take to develop continuous achievement through Inspirational Dissatisfaction.

—*W. Clement Stone*

Chapter Six

The Power of Progress Checks

Measuring Your Results

Success in selling should never be measured by what you are. It should be measured by what you are when compared to what you could be. Be a good student of yourself. Learn by frequent self-examination to appraise and improve your attitudes, skills, and effectiveness.

—Fred G. Holderman, Jr.

Don't Be A Grounded Eagle

An American Indian tells about a brave who found an eagle's egg and put it into the nest of a prairie chicken. The eaglet hatched with the brood of chicks and grew up with them. All his life, the eagle did what prairie chickens do. You see, the eagle thought he was a prairie chicken. He scratched in the dirt for seeds and insects to eat. He even clucked and cackled like a chicken. The eagle never flew more than a few feet off the ground. After all, that's how prairie chickens were intended to fly. The years passed and the eagle grew old. One day he saw a magnificent bird far above him in the sky. It soared on the powerful wind currents, spiraling upward with scarcely a beat of its mighty wings.

"What a beautiful creature!" said the eagle to the prairie chicken next to him. "What is it?"

"That's an eagle, the chief of the birds," the other bird responded. "But, don't give a thought to emulating him. You could never soar that high."

The eagle was convinced. He never gave it another thought. And he died thinking he was a prairie chicken.

What a waste of potential! That bird was built to rule the heavens, but conditioned to stay earthbound. He pecked at stray seeds and chased insects. Though he was designed to be among the most awesome of all birds, he believed in his neighbor's example and counsel: "You're only a prairie chicken—go find some insects."

You may find yourself in a situation much like that of the eagle. You feel as though you are designed to perform in a superior way. At times, you feel you have the ability and experience to move beyond your present self-imposed limitations. But for some reason, you choose to be influenced by what others say or what they do. *Winning means excelling at being yourself.* You have the right to win, to "soar," to make plans, to see those plans fulfilled, to become the best you that you can possibly become. Larry Wilson, the well-known Minneapolis consultant, says it this way: "Professionals are not only good at what they do, but they know why they are good. Because they know they're good, they consistently check their progress and critique their own performances. Naturally, they continue to grow and become better." Checking the progress toward your goals and regularly critiquing your performance will cause you to "soar with the eagles" in the business of selling.

The Lou Behr Philosophy

One of the great names in the insurance history book is that of Lou Behr. A highly successful general agent in Chicago's Loop, Lou died while still a young man. But before that unfortunate event, he built a sales organization that was the envy of all managers. The agent productivity in the Behr organization was always impressively high. Lou believed a commitment to his four-step philosophy was a virtual guarantee for each of his associates to be and stay at their best. His four steps were:

1. *Wake up each day employed.* You do this by planning your selling day and its activities the previous day. First develop a complete "to do" list. Study it. Then rewrite the list, putting the things to be done in the order of their importance.

2. *Join the "seven-o'clock club."* Begin each day by studying to learn something new about your product or how you sell it.
3. *Meet three new people each day.* The insurance business is a contact business. Widening your prospect base each day sets you up for consistent activity.
4. *Complete and study a progress report each week.* At the end of each week, monitor your activity and measure your results.

The fourth step in the Lou Behr philosophy is our focus in this chapter.

The Progress Guide

Honest, intelligent effort is always rewarded in selling. That's the law of laws. *Monitoring activity and measuring results always improves upon those rewards.* You need a system of checkups to stay informed of your progress. Just as a scoreboard tells the players, coaches, and fans the score and how much time is left to win, so will a system of weekly check-ups gauge your progress. This is why we said in an earlier chapter that your goals must be measurable and have deadlines. Those factors are essential to the achievement of goals.

Your company may provide you a weekly report form similar to the one shown in Figure 6-1, the Progress Guide. Whatever form you use, it's important that you keep such a report each week. Discipline yourself to not only complete but study your progress in detail at the end of each week. Calculate the activity and production results you must make happen each week for the balance of the year to reach and surpass your important goals. When you do, "staying on top" of your business and selling at your best becomes a matter of focusing on high-payoff activities. It also produces consistency—and in selling, consistency produces satisfying results. This is the "ownership benefit" in keeping weekly records of your progress.

Selling Up to Your Potential

One of the most difficult jobs for you to tackle is that of completing an impartial, objective self-analysis. It's human nature to back off from any-

Figure 6-1

Progress Guide

Performance Today Is The
Key To The Future

Name _____

For week Ending_____ 19_____

No. of Weeks Worked This Year to Date_____

No. of Weeks Left to Work This Year _____

Activity and Production

	Total This Week	Total Last Week	Total Year To-Date	This Year's Goals	Yet To Go	Need Each Week
Life Insurance Pre-Approach Calls						
Opening Interviews						
Closing Interviews						
Life Paid Cases						
Commissions						
MDRT Credits						
Referred Leads						
Disability and Health Commissions						
Equity Commissions						
Group Commissions						

Records To Break

Most Paid Cases in a month _____

Largest Case Sold $ _____

Most MDRT Credits in a month $____

Honest, Intelligent Effort Is Always Rewarded.

thing that might puncture your ego. However, much good in the way of personal growth comes to those agents who engage in regular self-analysis. The worksheets on pages 170 through 176 help you evaluate yourself as an agent. On the worksheet, Selling Up to Your Potential, you can record your overall evaluations. In each column, mark a dot to show the rating you gave yourself for that topic. Next, draw a line from each dot to the next one. This graph will show you your strengths and reveal your weaknesses. You'll know what to work on and what to strengthen to make yourself a more effective agent.

Compete—Don't Compare

If you want to get on with this business of becoming the very best agent you possibly can, you need to turn your attention to what you are doing. *Think about the things you wish to achieve. Focus on doing the things that will cause you to "soar."* Don't be influenced by what others say or "conditioned" by what they have or haven't done. Let them have whatever they want. Let them do whatever they want to do. You're not in competition with them. You're in competition with yourself—your own talents, your own goals and standards. This is the competition whose reward is the greatest. The "constant struggle" is between what you are and what you are capable of becoming. Compete but don't compare!

A Final Measurement

Maybe you saw the news item some time back about a Canadian farmer who sold his Stradivarius violin for something like sixty thousand dollars. Our good friend, Earl Nightingale, brought it to our attention on one of his radio programs.

Antonio Stradivari, the Italian violin maker, lived from 1644 to 1737. That's ninety-three years at a time when the average life expectancy was around thirty. He worked alone, although later in his life his sons helped him. No committee advised him, no one made decisions for him. His tools were primitive, but that was not important. *He put himself into his work.* All the world's tools couldn't make up for that important ingredient. When

Selling Up to Your Potential—Do I Look Like a Successful Agent?

Rate yourself: Check YES or NO for each question.

	YES	NO
1. When I call on a prospect do I look like a successful agent?	_____	_____
2. Do I look confident, as though I know I can bring my prospect information and ideas he or she will be glad to have?	_____	_____
3. Do I walk and stand erect?	_____	_____
4. Do I follow a careful diet and keep myself trim?	_____	_____
5. Do I look alert, enthusiastic, and healthy?	_____	_____
6. Do I always have well-groomed hair, clean hands and fingernails, so that nothing about me distracts my prospect?	_____	_____
7. Are the colors of my wearing apparel businesslike?	_____	_____
8. Do I appear poised when I'm with a prospect or customer, never tense or anxious?	_____	_____
9. Do I avoid nervous hand habits such as adjusting my glasses, rubbing my nose, scratching my head, bending paper clips, etc.?	_____	_____
10. Do I display charisma and positiveness?	_____	_____

How to rate yourself on this subject: Add your NO answers and multiply by 10. Deduct that total from 100. For example: If you've checked the NO column 3 times, multiply 3 by 10 for a total of 30. Deduct 30 from 100, and you get a rating of 70 percent on this subject matter.

RATING _____ DATE _____

Selling Up to Your Potential — Do I Really Know What I'm Talking About?

Rate yourself: Check YES or NO for each question.

	YES	NO
1. Do I study on a regular basis to build my competence?		
2. Do prospects and clients consider me an authority?		
3. Do I know at least three good reasons why a prospect should want to buy what I am recommending?		
4. Do I know what my competitors are selling?		
5. Do I know why it would be more advantageous for my prospect to buy from me than from the competition?		
6. Do I know all about the products and services of my company?		
7. Do I know the advertising program that supports my selling efforts?		
8. Do I read business publications to keep informed about trends that might affect insurance and equity sales?		
9. Do I study the sales literature and listen to cassettes on a regular basis?		
10. Do I consistently search for ideas and information that might be helpful to my clients, or might help me serve them more effectively?		

How to rate yourself on this subject: Add your NO answers, multiply by 10, deduct from 100.

RATING _____ DATE _____

171

Selling Up to Your Potential—Do I Function Like a Professional Agent?

Only a fair and honest personal rating will enable you to discover your strong points and any weaknesses you want to strengthen. Reflect upon this week's sales interviews.

Rate yourself: Check YES or NO for each question.

	YES	NO
1. Am I proud to be in selling?	_____	_____
2. Do I try to improve my ability to communicate my ideas to prospects and clients more effectively?	_____	_____
3. Do I display confidence and enthusiasm which show in words and actions?	_____	_____
4. Is my speed of delivery neither too fast nor too slow?	_____	_____
5. Are my statements clear and not vague?	_____	_____
6. Do I eliminate distractors such as "and-ah," "er," "Do you see what I mean?" and, "you know"?	_____	_____
7. Do I do my homework and keep informed so that I am able to answer questions intelligently?	_____	_____
8. Do I build the trust level and my credibility right from the start?	_____	_____
9. Do I try to get everything I can out of sales meetings? Do I try to contribute as much as I can to the success of those meetings?	_____	_____
10. Do I try to increase my success by (1) analyzing my own work each week, and (2) planning a systematic self-improvement program?	_____	_____

How to rate yourself on this subject: Add your NO answers, multiply by 10, deduct from 100.

RATING _____ DATE _____

Selling Up to Your Potential — How Skillfully Do I Sell?

Rate yourself: Check YES or NO for each question.

	YES	NO
1. Do I learn as much as I can about my prospect before I call?	_____	_____
2. Do I start each interview by discussing something I know will interest my prospect?	_____	_____
3. Do I thoroughly understand what motivates people to buy?	_____	_____
4. Do I speak the prospect's language?	_____	_____
5. Do I always present my recommendations with an emphasis on the owner benefits?	_____	_____
6. Do I use sales-support materials effectively?	_____	_____
7. Is my explanation interesting and informative?	_____	_____
8. Do I present my story concisely and to the point?	_____	_____
9. Is my sales talk clear and easily understood?	_____	_____
10. Am I using words and phrases that inspire belief and gain understanding?	_____	_____

How to rate yourself on this subject: Add your NO answers, multiply by 10, deduct from 100.

RATING _____ DATE _____

---

he finished with an instrument—*when he was sure that his work measured up to his own personal standards*—he signed his name to it. And today, more than two hundred years later, his name is a household word all over the world.

What is it that causes one agent to take pride in what he or she does while others give little or no thought to the quality of their work? Do you know? Of course, when we talk about Stradivari, da Vinci, Carnegie, or Ford we're talking about great geniuses. These are exceptional talents who

Selling Up to Your Potential—How Successful are my Human Relations?

Rate yourself: Check YES or NO for each question.

	YES	NO
1. Do I learn the name of each prospect, address him or her by name, and use the name from time to time during my sales presentation?	_____	_____
2. Do I remember the names of everyone in a client's organization with whom I come in contact?	_____	_____
3. Am I well mannered and courteous?	_____	_____
4. Am I sincere? Do I avoid untruthfulness or exaggerations?	_____	_____
5. Am I a good listener? Do I listen without interrupting?	_____	_____
6. Do I creatively personalize my suggestions so prospects and clients know I care?	_____	_____
7. Am I reliable? Do I keep my promises? Do I deliver as promised? Am I punctual? Do I return telephone calls promptly?	_____	_____
8. Do I resist the temptation to talk about myself?	_____	_____
9. Do I always say "Thank you!" for sales and referrals?	_____	_____
10. Do I remember birthdays, anniversaries, other important occasions, and send a card or note to let my clients and associates know I remembered?	_____	_____

How to rate yourself on this subject: Add your NO answers, multiply by 10, deduct from 100.

RATING _____ DATE _____

Selling Up to Your Potential—How Effectively do I Control my Emotions?

Rate yourself: Check YES or NO for each question.

	YES	NO
1. Do I try not to lose my poise, even if I think a prospect or client treats me unfairly?	_____	_____
2. Do I accept responsibility for my own success and never blame "unreasonable prospects," "unfair competitors," or anything else for my failure to make sales?	_____	_____
3. Do I refuse to feel sorry for myself when I have a bad day and instead analyze my utilization of time to determine how it could be improved?	_____	_____
4. When I begin to doubt my own ability to sell, do I review my selling successes and stay determined to repeat them?	_____	_____
5. Do I try to keep my mind free from worry and replace negative thinking with positive thoughts of success and how it can be achieved?	_____	_____
6. Do I face problems and solve them instead of ignoring them and letting them become insurmountable?	_____	_____
7. Can I accept and profit from feedback that is critical but constructive?	_____	_____
8. Do I handle necessary but less challenging details of my work promptly and efficiently?	_____	_____
9. Do I start each day with an optimistic estimate of the sales activity I'm going to have?	_____	_____
10. Do I analyze my own reactions from time to time? Do I try to understand myself so I can keep my emotions under control more successfully?	_____	_____

How to rate yourself on this subject: Add your NO answers, multiply by 10, deduct from 100.

RATING _____ DATE _____

Selling Up to Your Potential										
Percentage Scale	10	20	30	40	50	60	70	80	90	100
Do I Look Like a Successful Agent?										
Do I Really Know What I'm Talking About?										
Do I Function Like a Professional?										
How Skillfully Do I Sell?										
How Successful are My Human Relations?										
How Effectively Do I Control My Emotions?										

found their niche and became great. There have been many other fine violin makers, artists, and producers who took just as much pride and care in their work, but lacked the same quality of talent. Even today, there are many thousands of craftsmen who will not turn out shoddy work—who are proud "to sign their names" to their own creations. They're in the minority, perhaps. But they've always been in the minority. *Acknowledgment of quality never changes*. Quality still commands the highest price. It's always recognized and respected wherever it's found. Agents who stamp excellence on their work gain two extra dividends: First, they build a following—*their clients come back*. Second, they have the satisfaction of becoming known as uncommon agents, *real professionals*.

In chapter 1 we referred to Albert E. N. Gray's important discovery. You'll remember, after searching for the common denominator of success, he concluded that the secret of every agent who has ever been successful lies in the fact that he or she formed the habit of doing the things failures won't do or can't do. Gray said, "Every single qualification for achieving unusual success is acquired through habits." You form habits and habits shape careers. If you do not deliberately form good habits, then unconsciously you form bad ones.

Monitoring activity, measuring results, and keeping your personal standards high are the kind of habits that move you to the top—and keep you there!

Chapter Six Flashbacks

1. An eagle is built to soar into the heavens, but can be _____to stay earthbound.

2. Winning in selling means _____at being yourself. Professionals consistently check their _____and critique their _____.

3. Simply stated, the Lou Behr philosophy is to
   a. wake up each day _____
   b. join the " _____ club"
   c. meet _____ new people each day.
   d. complete and study a _____ report each week.

4. Honest, _____ effort is always rewarded.

5. "Staying on top" of your business and selling at your best becomes a matter of focusing on _____ activities and measuring your _____ weekly.

6. To function like a professional agent, display _____ and _____and let it show in your words and actions.

7. To sell skillfully, keep the emphasis on _____ _____.

8. The "constant struggle" is between what you are and what you are capable of becoming. _____ but don't compare!

9. The respect for _____never changes. You gain two important dividends by stamping your work with excellence: you build a _____and you have the _____ of being a real professional.

10. Monitoring _____ , measuring _____ , and keeping your personal _____high are the kind of habits that move you to the top—and keep you there!

For answers see page 236.

Self-Motivators for Improving Measurement of Results

Amateurs make empty promises, professionals make commitments.

Amateurs criticize conditions, professionals change circumstances.

Amateurs judge themselves by minimum standards, professionals judge themselves by standards of excellence.

Think about each of these guidelines as you review your results each week. Make a habit of doing so at a regular time and in a situation in which you can reflect and think. Remember:

You don't always get what you expect *unless you* inspect *with regularity.*

Competence comes from study and practice; from competence comes reputation; from reputation, wealth and the true riches of life. So let study and practice be your guide.

Have you filled the last minute with sixty seconds full of distance run?

Make yourself your own toughest competitor.

Compete against others, but don't compare yourself to them.

Aim high!

A man's reach should exceed his grasp, or what's a heaven for?

Services rendered is the best rule by which to measure a day's work, or a lifetime's.

Hold yourself responsible for a higher standard than anybody else expects of you. Never excuse yourself. Never pity yourself. Be a hard taskmaster to yourself.

—Henry Ward Beecher

Commentary: How to Develop Persistence

I was once asked this question: "How can a person develop enough persistence to allow him to persist long enough to develop the habit of persistence?"

It's a question that every sales rep should be able to answer if he or she wants to achieve enduring success—in sales, and in personal life. Let's not talk about the sale. Let's confine our discussion to the question.

During the late twenties, almost anyone could sell almost anything, just as they can today. Because of boom times, salesmen with pleasing personalities, then as now, could make large sales and profits without paying the price to learn and apply the best techniques and develop the best selling skills. Then, as now, if they lost one selling job, they could get another.

Failure of Attitudes

But in 1930 many of the financially successful salesmen of the previous decade became "has-beens." Their negative mental attitudes had never been changed to positive ones. At the same time, there were other salesmen of character who were motivated, through necessity, to strive to earn their livelihoods for their familes, pay off their debts, and achieve enduring success. Because of a burning desire to succeed, they kept on trying, and thus they developed the habit of persistence by striving day by day to do better. The habit became ingrained, and they didn't lose it.

179

To an honest man, necessity is a motivating factor that forces him to keep on trying—to continue to persist. For while success is achieved by those who try, *enduring success is achieved by those who KEEP trying*.

Prosperous times have now been experienced in the United States for such a long period that many sales reps who once were financially successful are becoming "has-beens" even without the push of a decline in the economy. Like many of the salespeople in the twenties, they are failing to prepare themselves for the future.

It's quite common today to see sales reps who once struggled to earn good incomes, and, once having attained that goal, begin to deviate from the principles that brought about their success. They have already reached the heights of their selling careers and earning power, and—though they don't realize it—they are on the decline.

But you don't need a depression, a catastrophe, or other necessity to motivate you to develop enough persistence. (Or do you?) You don't need to be starving to be motivated to strive and struggle for continuing success in achieving worthwhile objectives. (Or do you?) You don't need a sales manager, your wife, or any other person to force you to develop an intense, eager, burning desire to make the most of the unusual opportunities that are available to you as a salesperson in America today. (Or do you?) If you do, you are on your way to becoming a "has-been" . . . if you have not already arrived there.

How to Develop Enough Persistence

Now the man who asked me the question at the beginning of this commentary is not a "has-been." In fact, he is not a salesman or sales manager by vocation. He is in the mental health field, trying to prevent mental illness and bring about mental health for those who are in need. The question was asked in good faith, and it got me thinking. Also, it motivated me to act.

During the year that followed, I endeavored to motivate the salesmen and sales managers in my companies to go back to the basic principles that made my organization a success.

I recommended to them, as I am now recommending to you, that they read self-help books and apply the principles they contain, if they want to develop the habit of persistence. For persistence is needed to achieve enduring success.

The principle used by Alcoholics Anonymous is a good one to apply: *take one day at a time.*

Keep your objective in mind for just one day. Then the next day start a new day, and keep your objective before you. Now anyone can go one day in the development of a good new habit or the elimination of an old, undesirable one.

Persistent sales reps set an objective for their entire program. Then, specific objectives for each day. They think about, talk about, and keep their objectives ever before them. Many pray for guidance.

These winners develop many personal techniques that are helpful, such as reading their resolutions each and every morning, having self-motivators (a good one is: *Be persistent!*) pasted around their homes to remind them of their objectives, and repeating these self-motivators aloud fifty or a hundred times every morning and fifty or a hundred times every evening: *Be persistent! Be persistent!*

Does it work? Of course if works. I know of a salesman who responded to the book *I Dare You!* He was an alcoholic, but he persisted day by day. He took one day at a time, and the battle took ten years. But he won. He increased his sales and earnings. Today he is a wealthy man. For his mind was clear enough to invest wisely. He set objectives in sales and the acquisition of wealth.

Have Courage to Face the Truth

That man won and became successful because he had courage to face the truth. This is something you must do also in order to be persistent.

Have courage to face the truth. Pay the price immediately. A delay may only be a deferred payment with penalties compounded until they become ruinous.

Have courage to face the truth when

1. You have that strong "guilt feeling." (Stand up to it now . . . waiting will make it worse.)

181

2. You are on the wrong track or headed in the wrong direction. (Stop as soon as possible—regardless of how far you have traveled, it is never too late! Do it now!)
3. You have tried to solve your problems unsuccessfully and need outside help. (Get it!)
4. You have an unpleasant or distasteful duty. (Perform it!)

How will you see the truth when you are blinded by your own feelings and emotions? One good method is to seek advice from those who honestly want and have the ability to help you—whether they be a clergyman, doctor, psychiatrist, close relative, or employer. The person you choose should be someone who you feel is in a position to evaluate you and your problem accurately and who, at the same time, will tell you what you should listen to, even though it may be unpleasant or shocking to you.

Be prepared to disclose all the facts, if necessary. Be prepared to listen with an open mind. Be prepared to follow through with action.

When you see the truth, how can you develop the courage to pay the price immediately? Here's how:

1. *Make the exhortation* Do it now! *a part of yourself.* And get into action every time you use it!
2. *Weld hope to you.* Know that a right solution can and will be found if you keep trying.
3. *Pray for the desired results.*

As Tyrell Griffin once pointed out, most of us will do the heroic thing in an emergency situation. It is in the daily battle with "little" things that we lack courage. But it is precisely there that one must strive for victory, knowing that success in achieving anything is not realized overnight but in the sum of hours, days, and years of endeavor. Griffin quoted this homily:

Wealth lost, something lost;
Honor lost, much lost;
Courage lost, ALL lost!

Have courage to face the truth and rise above the problems it presents. Remember, persistent people begin their success where others end in failure.

—*W. Clement Stone*

Chapter Seven
The Power of Persistence
Staying At Your Best

You've got a life to live. It's short, at best. It's a wonderful privilege and a terrific opportunity—and you've been equipped for it. Use your equipment, give it all you've got, trust God, work hard and don't quit.

—Norman Vincent Peale

A Most Valuable Asset

Gabriela Andersen-Scheiss, a thirty-nine-year-old runner from Switzerland, demonstrated the meaning of persistence to the entire world in her dramatic finish of the marathon in the 1984 Olympic Games in Los Angeles.

She had no hope of earning a medal. Her body's tissues were desiccated from the hours of running under a pitiless sun, and she'd fallen twenty minutes behind the leaders. Thirty runners had already completed the 26–mile, 385–yard event when Gabriela came lurching through the tunnel and into the coliseum.

The seventy thousand spectators went to their feet to cheer her on as she staggered in a weaving half-run around the arena. It took five agonizing minutes for her to complete the final lap.

When she finally crossed the finish line and collapsed into the arms of the doctors, the ovation she received was louder and more sustained than the one that had been given to Joan Benoit, the winner of the Gold Medal. The spectators recognized that, even though Gabriela came in thirty-seventh, she was a winner.

What relationship does that pain-wracked, dehydrated woman's struggle to finish her race bear to your performance as an agent?

Plenty!

You are in a race every bit as demanding as a marathon. The conditions are totally different, of course. The crowd that will cheer you on at the end may be small, or even nonexistent. But you must keep running, day after day, even when there's no hope of getting a medal.

Why?

Because, like Gabriela Andersen-Scheiss, you don't have to be among the top three to be a winner. You simply have to do your best every step of the way and *finish* as well as you can. For as the oft-repeated homily attributed to Calvin Coolidge puts it:

Nothing else in the world can take the place of persistence. Talent will not; nothing is more common than unsuccessful people with talent. Genius will not; unrewarded genius is almost a proverb. Education will not; the world is full of educated derelicts. Persistence and determination alone are omnipotent.

Study the history of any agent who achieves consistent, high-level production, and you will find that persistence played a major role in his or her success. When Fred Novy was a beginning agent in Chicago, he found it difficult to believe that the people he approached would actually purchase policies from him. As a result, he gave up easily and failed to close many sales.

One day he was invited to the suburban home of his vice-president, who apparently thought Fred had a lot of promise and was concerned about his poor sales results. They talked about the problem, and the vice-president counseled Fred to learn to persist. He pointed out Calvin Coolidge's homily, which was inscribed on a plaque that hung in his den. It was prefaced by these words: "Persistence . . . is a most valuable asset. Individuals who have and use this quality always get somewhere."

As a result of that visit, Fred made two decisions. First, he told himself that he would not consider a week's work finished until he had made at least fifty new calls. A new call, according to his self-imposed definition, would be someone to whom he'd never before talked on the subject of insurance. Second, he decided he would become so successful in selling life insurance that one day he could afford to live in the same neighborhood as his vice-president and own the same kind of home.

Once he made up his mind on those two things—demonstrating the willingness to pay the price for a definite goal—Fred Novy turned a record of failure into one of success. Which is no surprise, for success consistently follows a made-up mind.

In the course of doggedly completing his fifty new calls each day, Fred talked to an official of the Art Institute of Chicago. The individual didn't want any more insurance; but during the conversation he happened to mention that the school of the Art Institute was considering a change in its group coverage. Fred called his company's group rep, and the two of them made a presentation to the Art Institute's administrators.

The sale was made, and Fred has since done such an outstanding job of servicing the school of the Art Institute that he has been elected to the board of governors of that prestigious institution. His success in the field of life insurance also has allowed him to become one of the Art Institute's most valued donors. And, yes, he and his family now live in the suburbs—directly across the street from that vice-president's home.

Og Mandino once told the story of an obnoxious newspaper columnist who interviewed one of the leading life-insurance agents in the United States, a stocky, balding, permanent member of the Life Underwriter's Million Dollar Round Table. She thought she would "needle" him a bit and perhaps get a story.

"How do you explain your luck in selling more than a million dollars a year?" she asked.

The agent studied her face for a moment, reached into his jacket pocket, and withdrew a white, folded document.

"This is a signed application for two-hundred fifty thousand dollars worth of life insurance that I sold to a client this morning," he said. "Do you see these four pencil marks in the upper border of the application?"

She nodded, frowning, and waited for him to continue.

"When I am trying to persuade a prospect that he needs more coverage, I don't give up until I have asked him five times. Every time I ask and he says no, I put one of these small pencil marks in the upper right-hand corner of the application. Then I review for him *again* all the benefits he would gain if he purchased the insurance. This may require a second, third, or fourth meeting. In any case, I keep calling on him until I have asked him five times."

The columnist looked disappointed and a bit puzzled.

"My prospect will nearly always say yes, before I have asked for the fifth time," the agent explained with a broad smile. "My success, such as it is, has never been a matter of *luck* . . . only persistence."

The Anatomy of Persistence

Let's examine this invaluable trait of persistence. Here are its three elements:

1. *Definiteness of Purpose*—Knowing what you want is the first and perhaps the most important step toward developing persistence. Again, reduce to writing your definite chief aim. A strong motive forces you to do whatever it takes to overcome difficulties. What you foresee is what you get!

2. *Burning Desire*—The desire to improve your professional status as an agent must be great. Before you can approach your goal, you must want to get there, and this desire must be genuine. *The best way to build your desire is to consistently visualize the gains to be made.* If you'd like, think of them as financial gains. Picture the commissions you intend to earn. Visualize the higher standard of living these earnings will make possible. Linking rewards with personal growth, not just the money itself, is a powerful motivator. Set your goals high. Picture them often. *The result will be action—determined, intelligent action.*

The majority of your competitors will be ready to throw their aims and purposes overboard and give up at the first sign of opposition or disappointment. Only a few carry on against all obstacles until they attain their goals.

There may be no heroic connotation to the word *persistence*, but the quality is to the character of an agent what carbon is to steel.

Your creative mind and "inner power" respond to strong emotion. Feed them with desire—a burning desire—and they will serve you well. You'll find yourself studying your performance easily and with enthusiasm.

Concentration will come naturally. *Your subconscious mind will respond by directing you to do the things that will insure your selling success.*

3. *Habits* — Persistence and habit are interactive. Good habits can only be developed through persistence and yet persistence itself can be developed into a habit. Your mind comprises your daily experiences. This is a cardinal rule of psychology. *Even fear, the worst of enemies for anyone in selling, can be cured by a forced repetition of courageous acts.* Habit, the natural repetition of any act or way of thinking, is an important factor in achieving success.

Tenacity is the hallmark of a persistent agent like Brenda Mahon, who is with Mass Mutual in Dallas. She says: "If I'm tenacious, it's because I do a good job of probing during an interview. *I develop facts but I also listen closely to the prospect's feelings.* I want to know what the real concerns are and what the prospect desires to achieve. In addition, I want to make certain what resources are available to handle the premium."

Brenda says she then employs "creative visualization." She creates a "vision" for each prospect. "Once that vision is crystal clear in my mind, I begin to conceptualize how I can best solve the problem and reach the prospect's goal," she says. "My aim is not just to make a sale, but to satisfy the prospect's desires.

"Working through this type of thought process keeps me persistent until the sale is closed," she adds. "I'm determined not to give up too soon. If I do, there's the chance that a more persistent agent will come along and close 'my business' — or worse yet, nothing happens and the prospect has an inadequate plan or no plan at all.

"Without a 'vision' nothing much happens," Brenda concludes. "With it, I have the courage to stick and stay until the job is done."

Insurance Against Failure

The agent who develops the habit of persistence enjoys a high degree of insurance against failure. This agent *simply refuses to acknowledge failure.* No matter how many setbacks this agent meets, he or she still manages to reach the top of the sales honor roll. Persistence always wins out. There's no substitute for persistence. It cannot be supplanted by genius or luck. Remember this and you'll have the strongest of motives for developing the habit of persistence.

Take inventory of yourself. Study the elements of persistence and determine how well you are developing them. Measure yourself objectively. There can be no permanent defeat unless you accept it. There is really no insurmountable barrier except an inherent weakness of purpose.

Persistent agents generally have strong needs for recognition and prestige. They try to make things happen fast and they believe making money is an important "measuring rod" in their careers. *Keep in mind, highly persistent agents aren't necessarily successful, but most successful agents are highly persistent.*

The Mickey Mantle Theory

The people who are the most successful in life are those who not only do not fear failure but often fail repeatedly before or while achieving their goals. Mickey Mantle's test was strikeouts and walks, of which he had 1,710 and 1,734, respectively, during his career with the Yankees. "That's 3,444 times I came to bat without hitting the ball," Mickey said. "Figure 500 at-bats a season for a man playing regularly and that means I played seven years without hitting the ball." That's a lot of swings and misses, a lot of failures to connect, a lot of frustration at the plate for one of the most respected batting champions baseball has ever known.

But no one took much note of Mickey Mantle's failures. The Mick is best remembered for his leadership and his clutch hitting. Whatever your goals in selling might be, you will be more likely to achieve them if you're not afraid to fail. The Mantle Theory is that failure is nothing more than a stepping stone to success. Many psychotherapists agree that the individuals who fulfill their potential, who achieve the most out of their career, are those individuals who learn from their difficult moments and who "stay in there swinging."

Difficulties bring out your best qualities and make greatness possible. The superior performance in selling that you admire in another usually took place because the agent subscribed to what we might call the "It's too early to give up" philosophy.

188

Applying the Mantle Theory

Joe Gootter, a great agent based in Tucson, was a well-known actor on the "Phil Silvers Show" before he went into the insurance business. Joe says: "Acting is statistically the hardest profession in the world. In the insurance business, we are taught the law of averages. In show business, there is no such law. I could go to thirty casting agents and not get any results, not any parts. But in the insurance business you can manage your results statistically by demonstrating persistence and intelligent effort."

Joe developed "stick-to-it-iveness," the ability to press forward in both sales and education. He says, "You have to stick to it and persist every day of your business life. You must upgrade your activities. Remember, failures are people who refuse to do the things successful people form the habit of doing.

"There is no standoff with call reluctance or procrastination," Joe continues. "Either they beat you, or you beat them. I learned to defeat both of these enemies by putting a dollar value on a prospect's name. If I sold John a plan and earned a one-thousand-dollar commission, and John recommended me to three of his associates, potentially, each of John's referrals are worth one thousand dollars to me. But none of John's referrals are worth anything if I don't rout procrastination and overcome call reluctance with persistence. In other words, I must make contact with prospects. I can't keep the bat on my shoulder!"

Living in Balance

Over seventy years ago, the noted Harvard-trained philosopher and physician, Richard C. Cabot, wrote the book *What Men Live By*. In it he explored the elements of a balanced life: work, play, love, and worship. Although the book has been out of print and many of the references seem archaic, the basic principles have stood the test of time.

There is a need in all of us to be productive, to enjoy daily life, to be energetic, to have people in our lives that we care about and to extend our interests beyond ourselves. *Too much or too little of any of these things can set our lives out of balance, destroy our sense of self-worth or dull our enjoyment of life.*

The Power of Persistence

A number of Persistence Disposition Questionnaires (PDQs) have been devised to measure this trait. One such instrument was devised by B.N. Mukherjee when he was professor of psychology at York University in Toronto. The items in the quiz shown are adapted from his research.

Exhibit 7-1 – Rating Your Persistence

To learn what your Persistence Index is, answer each statement true or false, then read on for explanations.

1. Little can be gained by people who attempt to do things that are too difficult for them.

2. Compared with others, I hate to lose at anything.

3. The stronger the chance of failing at something, the less determined I am to keep at it.

4. I am known to be a stickler for fighting for my rights.

5. It's better to accomplish many easy jobs than to attempt a few that are very difficult.

6. Luck is an important factor in determining whether one succeeds.

7. Compared with others, I set high goals for myself.

8. People who get ahead work only with their heads rather than with their hands.

9. Regardless of whether I work for myself or someone else, there's no change in my level of ambition.

10. I procrastinate more than my friends when faced with an unpleasant job.

SCORING: Answers: 1.F; 2.T; 3.F; 4.T; 5.F; 6.F; 7.T; 8.T, 9.F; 10.F.
Give yourself 1 point for each of your answers that correspond with those given in the answer key.

If you scored: 8–10 points, you are a highly persistent agent; 4–7 points, you are probably an individual with an average degree of persistence; 0–3 points, you are low on persistence for one engaged in sales, you give up too easily. When things become difficult, decide to stick it out. You may be surprised to discover that a little more effort can yield results more positive than you'd thought possible.

The Power of Persistence

Some years ago, Dr. George W. Crane, a professor at Northwestern University, developed the concept that each person carries throughout his or her career a "Cross of Life."* This cross has five dimensions: professional, physical, financial, personal, and spiritual. When these elements are in balance, a person can function at full capacity. Dr. Crane feels that far too many people manage to fail for reasons that have nothing to do with the way they perform their jobs. He says: "They simply get their 'Cross of Life' out of balance."

Let's examine each dimension of the "Cross" so you can determine for yourself the kinds of habits you should be developing.

- Professional Growth—It's impossible to put a price tag on professional competence, because the payoff for it is far more than extra dollars earned. *It involves such intangibles as personal satisfaction, enjoyment of your work, and stature as a person.* If you're the average agent, you put in a fifty-hour week, more or less. This leaves you with about sixty-two hours a week, or about twice the time spent on the job, when you are neither working nor sleeping. This is more than enough time to follow programs designed to increase your knowledge of the business and methods that will improve your effectiveness. If you devote only one hour a day to this kind of investment in yourself, it will still leave you about sixty hours a week for leisure activities. This single hour a day can also make you an authority as an agent in five years or less.

Your company would soon go broke if it failed to "plow back" a certain percentage of its profits into research and development—seeking ways and means of making it a better company. How much of your income do you intend to "plow back" into your own research and development department, your own professional growth?

---

*The "Cross of Life" has an interesting history behind it. The Kinders credit Dr. Crane, the Northwestern University psychology professor, with the concept. However, Dr. Crane was probably introduced to the Cross by Dr. William Kepler of the Mayo Clinic, who in turn learned it from Dr. Hugh Cabot, another prominent Mayo physician, the older brother of Richard Cabot.

The motto of a prominent Chicago advertising agency reads: *"Where only the best is good enough."* What a motto this can be for your career as a professional agent! Adopt it as your own. Hang it up in your bedroom. Display it in your office. Carry it with you in your billfold,' weave it into the texture of everything you do, and your sales work is sure to become what you want it to be—a masterpiece.

There's an invisible element of superiority added to the character of the agent who consciously puts the trademark of quality on his or her work. The mental and moral effect of doing things accurately, conscientiously, and thoroughly can hardly be estimated because the processes are so gradual, so subtle. *Every time you obey the inward law of doing right, you hear an inward approval.* On the contrary, every half-done, careless, slipshod job that goes out of your hands leaves its trace of demoralization behind, and excellence becomes impossible. Much has been written in recent years about the business effectiveness of the Japanese. They feel a sense of achievement in their work and pride in their productivity. In your selling career, you will like yourself much better when you have the approval of your conscience.

There is no other advertisement for the agent like a good reputation. Many of America's greatest manufacturers have regarded their reputation as their most precious possession, and under no circumstances would they allow their names to be put on an imperfect article. Large sums of money are often paid for the use of a name because of its reputation for integrity, reliability, and excellence.

There's nothing like being enamored of excellence. No other characteristic makes such a strong, lasting impression upon your clients. Never be satisfied with "fairly good," "pretty good," or "that's going to be O.K., I think." Do every selling job to a finish and accept nothing but your best every time. Someone is watching. Someone will notice. And that someone may become a valuable client.

Study exhibit 7-2, Peak-Performer Characteristics. You'll learn about the ten traits of top producers. These are the characteristics you'll want to develop to grow professionally.

Economist John W. Galbraith was asked the secret for consistently achieving excellence in your job. He said: "Whatever it is you do today, do it better tomorrow."

Exhibit 7-2—Peak-Performer Characteristics

Dr. Charles Garfield, of the University of California at Berkeley, has developed from his research the following ten traits of high achievers.

1. They have foresight and the ability to carry out strategic plans.

2. They demonstrate a drive toward transcending previous levels of accomplishment.

3. They possess high levels of confidence and self-worth.

4. They have a high need for responsibility and control.

5. They are effective communicators.

6. They utilize mental preparation for critical events or key situations.

7. They require little in the way of outside praise or recognition.

8. They show a tendency to take creative risks rather than getting stuck in a comfort zone.

9. They critique themselves and self-correct.

10. They take a proprietary attitude toward their job. They see the significance of their contribution.

Demand excellence of yourself. It attracts and builds credibility. Don't tolerate mediocrity. There's no room for compromise among professionals. Stamp your work with excellence; it's the stamp of the professional.

- *Physical Self*—The old saying: "If I'd known I was going to live so long, I would have taken better care of myself," is worth considering. People are living longer these days. The Bureau of Census predicts that by the year 2000 about one hundred thousand will be age one hundred or older. By 2050, there will be about one million centenarians.

If you plan to live a long and productive life, taking good care of yourself is very important. The work of an agent can be fulfilling, enjoyable, and productive at any age if you take good care of your health and stay active.

A regular exercise program, a healthy diet, and routine physical examinations can help you stay healthy and productive longer. As Dr. Kenneth Cooper says: "You can't store physical fitness." You must work to maintain it daily. *The agent with a high level of energy has a definite competitive edge.* Make certain you achieve and maintain that edge. See exhibit 7-3, How to Feel Better and Live Longer, to learn Mayo Clinic's recommended steps for achieving longer, healthier days.

This is a scientific, physical fitness rating procedure based on the intensity and duration of various kinds of exercise. It helps you achieve and maintain a high level of cardiovascular fitness.

Exhibit 7-3 — How to Feel Better and Live Longer

Each year two hundred thousand people find their way to the famed Mayo Clinic, searching for the secret of good health. The finest medical minds in the world offer the following steps for longer, healthier days:

1. *Protect yourself.* Longevity is up to the individual. Enormous gains have been made in life expectancy. At the turn of the century, the main killers were infectious diseases. Major killers today are cancer and heart disease. The alert individual can protect himself or herself from these disorders.

2. *Have a periodic medical checkup.* The crucial age is from forty to fifty. When you weather this dangerous decade, you are on your way to the eighties.

3. *Don't ignore symptoms.* The chances for curing an ailment are greatly improved by early detection.

4. *Reduce your weight steadily each year.* Fat agents seldom grow old.

5. *Stop smoking.* Patients are highly motivated to quit after a heart attack. Dr. John Juergen's specialty is hardening of the arteries. "I can do more by getting people to stop smoking than by surgery," he asserts.

6. *Watch out for alcohol.* Most people do not understand how quickly alcohol creeps in for the kill.

7. *Exercise regularly.* Exercise daily, preferably following a prescribed routine such as Cooper's aerobic point system. (This is a scientific scoring system.)

8. *Be optimistic.* You can will yourself to be ill or well.

9. *Take a vacation.* Get away from your work routinely.

10. *Have a positive attitude.* Believe that you can be healthy.

Following these recommendations might easily extend your own lifespan from ten to thirty years.

- *Financial Well-being* — This third dimension of the "Cross of Life," the condition of your financial balance sheet, is generally a reliable measurement of the balance you are achieving in your life.

One of the most worthwhile exercises for improving your financial position is drawing up a "Living Will." Unlike an ordinary last will and testament, which makes certain that your financial matters are handled when you die in the manner you wished them to be, the "Living Will" is a document that sets forth how you want your finances managed during your lifetime. It's really a long-range goal-setting exercise, but doing it in the form of a will may make the objectives much more meaningful. It may help you internalize the truth that we pass this way but once, and that the only way to achieve future goals is through present planning and action. It should bring home to you the importance of regularly reviewing the material in chapter 3.

Every agent has the right to decide what kind of person he or she will become. You determine what income level you wish to attain, and what you would like your net worth to be. This is your business and yours alone. *But never be satisfied with a personal "balance sheet" that is anything less than you want it to be.*

Personal budget-keeping is back in style. It's increasingly essential to getting the maximum benefit from your selling income and to protecting your savings. Don't rely entirely on your instinctive sense of money management. Get a statistical handle on your living and business expenses, along with your anticipated commission earnings. Develop a plan of control over your spending. You will then make progress toward the kind of life-style that means the most to you.

- *Personal Life* — For most, this means the "quality time" spent with the members of one's family. As an agent, you're sure to discover the difficulty of scheduling such time with them. But you cannot separate family plans from your personal development. Discuss your business and your goals with your family. Talk freely about your accomplishments and demonstrate a positive attitude toward your selling job and its future. Unfortunately, we've found that some agents use the audience at home as a "sounding board" for business-related problems and complaints. *You'll discover a tremendous asset in your family's morale when you share with them the meaning and successes of your work.*

Dr. George W. Comstock of Johns Hopkins School of Hygiene and Public Health conducted studies of the relation of social and economic factors to disease among the population of Washington County, Maryland. He and his colleagues made an incidental but fascinating discovery: regular church-going and the clean living that often goes with a balanced family life appear to help people avoid a whole bagful of ailments. Among them, heart disease, cirrhosis of the liver, tuberculosis, cancer of the cervix, chronic bronchitis, fatal one-car accidents, and suicide. Comstock told *Time* magazine that this result proved that "Nice guys do, literally, finish last."

- *Spiritual*—Dr. Crane suggests that today most readers and students are searching for the "quick fix"—the mini-course, so to speak. He says it's this final dimension of "The Cross" that makes possible a "quick and reliable" way to achieve balance. The spiritual element provides a strong foundation for stability and purpose in both your professional and personal life. And this spiritual aspect touches and binds together each of the other dimensions. A spiritual element that is really a part of you will enable you to live a harmonious life. *Spiritual harmony will keep you well. It will fill you with strength, vitality, and optimism.*

Thomas Carlyle said: "It's the spiritual which always determines the material." This is one reason for focusing on the spiritual and growing in this important area. The spiritual can and will affect every other area of your personal and professional life in a very positive way.

Carlyle also said: "There's but one life—a little gleam of time between two vast eternities. No second chance for us, forever more."

That's reason enough to live in balance, isn't it?

Staying at Your Best

Our good friend and associate, Ray Calvert, talks to our sales clinic audiences about a hero he had as a young boy, growing up in the East. Ray's hero was the incomparable Babe Ruth.

Babe Ruth hit 714 home runs during his baseball career, but age caught up with him. The once-uncanny reflexes slowed, and the Babe was traded by the Yankees to the Boston Braves. One day the Braves were playing the Reds in an important game in Cincinnati. The great Babe Ruth demonstrated rather pathetically that he no longer was the effective player he had once been. He mishandled a ball; he threw badly; and in one inning alone, his errors led to five runs for the Reds.

As the Babe came off the field after the third out and headed for the dugout, a crescendo of "boos" greeted him. Just then, a boy jumped over the railing and onto the playing field. With tears streaming down his face, he threw his arms around the legs of his hero.

The hulking figure stooped slowly to stare down at the boy. Then he picked him up, hugged him, and set him down on his feet. Ruth patted the youngster's head, took his hand, and together they walked off the field.

The mood of the noisy, hostile crowd changed suddenly. There was no more booing. A hush fell over the stands. Then the silence was exploded by a deafening ovation.

In those brief moments, the fans saw two heroes—Babe Ruth, a "has-been" who still had the heart of a champion, and the small lad who cared about the feelings of another human being. Together, they demonstrated the essence of what it means to act courageously in the face of failure, to be your personal best.

Maximizing Your Potential

For uncounted years, the water at Niagara Falls dashed over the rocky cliffs, the power of millions of horses behind it. It was a beautiful sight for the occasional tourist, but nothing more. Today, that same Niagara turns the wheels of a hundred great industries and gives light and power to all of western New York. What made the difference? The Niagara has not changed—it had exactly the same power all the time. The difference is that science has shown us how to harness that power—how to use it effectively.

In the same way, this book has shown you how to use your own latent powers. We hope it has stirred the "sleeping giant" within you and already has made you far more effective in your selling role.

Most people are conditioned to believe that some individuals are born with sales ability and some without, and that those without must serve those who have it. Nothing could be further from the truth! Every agent is born with ability sufficient to master the art of professionalism in selling. *Everything necessary for becoming effective in selling can be acquired and developed.* All it takes is a responsible commitment, disciplined, consistent effort, and a results-focused attitude.

Above all, always bounce back. In selling, failure means very little if success comes eventually. *Resolve to perform what you should. Perform without fail that which you resolve.* Get up when you fall down. If you get in the game—stay in! The secret of success is constancy of purpose.

Say I Will

Our friend Tom Haggai makes reference to the persistence demonstrated by the members of Alcoholics Anonymous. One AA member, anonymous of course, compiled the following resolutions:

Just for today I will *try to live through this day only, and not be concerned with those far-reaching goals that would cause me to focus on all of my problems at once. I know I can do something for twelve hours that would discourage me if I felt I had to maintain it for a lifetime.*

Just for today I will *try to be happy. Abe Lincoln said, "Most folks are about as happy as they make up their mind to be." He was right. I will not dwell on thoughts that depress me. I will chase them out of my mind and replace them with positive thoughts.*

Just for today I will *adjust myself to what is. I will face reality. I will try to change those things I can change and accept those things I cannot change.*

Just for today I will improve my mind. I will not be a mental loafer. I will force myself to read something that requires effort, thought, and concentration.

Just for today I will do something I've been putting off. I will finally write the letter, make the call, or remove the clutter around me.

There is plenty of food for thought contained in those suggestions, and it all has to do with the building of persistence. Hannah Moe wrote, "The keen spirit seizes the prompt occasion. It makes the thought start into instant action and at once plans and performs, resolves, persists, and executes."

We conclude this book the way we started. *Your brain can make or break you! It takes in, digests, and gives meaning to your every experience.* It initiates and regulates your every thought, emotion, and action — conscious or unconscious.

If there is one truth, above all others, that you must recognize about yourself as an agent, it is this astounding fact: *"Nothing is either good or bad, but your thinking makes it so!"*

We believe the specific recommendations offered you at the end of each chapter can be "mental vitamins" that will keep your thinking healthy. Say *I will* revisit them regularly. Say *I will* inwardly digest them. Say *I will* make them a dominant part of my selling style.

If you do, you will have then discovered the secrets of successful insurance sales.

Good luck, and good selling!

Chapter Seven Flashbacks

1. The essential factor in the success formula is _____.
2. The first element of persistence is knowing _____ _____ _____.
3. The best way to build your desire is by "_____ _____."
4. Organized _____, even imperfect ones, encourage persistence.
5. Knowing that your plans are sound and based on _____ and _____ will encourage persistence.
6. The Mickey Mantle Theory encourages you to be willing to _____ repeatedly in order to achieve your selling goals and reach your potential.
7. Joe Gootter said you can manage your _____ statistically by demonstrating _____ of effort.
8. According to Dr. George W. Crane, successful people in sales often fail because they choose not to live their lives in _____.
9. The five dimensions in your "Cross of Life" are
   a. _____
   b. _____
   c. _____
   d. _____
   e. _____
10. Everything necessary for becoming effective in selling can be _____ and _____.

_____

See page 237 for answers.

Self-Motivators to Help You Stay at Your Best

"To really succeed in life," says Dr. Robert Schuller, founder and senior minister of the Crystal Cathedral in Garden Grove, California and author of many inspirational books, "all you have to do is (1) get started, and (2) never quit! These are the only two hurdles you need to clear to become the person you want to be."

Get started—that takes us back to the first chapter of this book. By now you know what PMA is, and you have learned how to develop a Positive Mental Attitude and how to maintain it when all about you seems negative. You've also written down your definite chief aim. You know how to proceed in your work as an agent, positioning yourself to make the sale, and doing it persuasively and professionally.

As you proceed toward your goals, visualize those objectives as if you had already attained them. Think of self-motivators that will help you persist, such as:

Success is achieved by those who try; enduring success is achieved by those who keep *trying.*

Be persistent!

Take one day at a time.

Have courage to face the truth.

Follow the Mickey Mantle Theory—don't be afraid to fail.

Keep your life in balance—stay professionally alert, physically strong, financially sound, and personally disciplined.

Overcome resistance with persistence.

The highest reward for your toil is not what you get for it, but what you become by it.

—John Ruskin

Appendix A

In Chapter Three, The Power of Positioning, we recommend the Summit Client Information File as a model for gathering full and complete information on a prospect. Sample SCIF questionnaires are shown on the following pages.

These information-gathering forms are designed for use with the Summit Financial Writer, a financial planning software program distributed by Summit Innovative Systems, Inc., One Grand Centre, Suite 211, Sherman, TX 75090. The software is for IBM and IBM-compatible computers.

The Financial Writer and similar programs allow you to input the data gathered from clients and generate a number of different reports such as financial statements, and projections for income-tax, cash-flow, and estate-planning. Such computer analysis can give your client a complete and accurate assessment of his or her financial position or needs, and can be invaluable to you as a sales tool.

Of course, such software is not inexpensive. Note also that there will be many situations where you will not find it practical or necessary to gather all the information called for in this appendix.

SUMMIT   FINANCIAL   WRITER

C L I E N T   I N F O R M A T I O N   M I S C E L L A N E O U S   I N F O R M A T I O N

Client

Tax Information:

Name: Jack L. Minor

Birthplace: New York

Birth Date 03 / 14 / 54

Soc. Sec. # 635 / 34 / 1095

Occupation: Salesperson

Emply/Bus: Roberts Mfg.

Address: 2305 Sunset Dr.

City: Houston

State: Tx.   ZIP: 77071

Bus. Phone: (714) 569-7304 -

	Planning Years	1987	1988	1989
No. of Exemptions	4	4	4

Filing Status*   2   2   2
  *1 - Single   3 - Married/Sep.
   2 - Married/Jt.   4 - Head Hsld.

Year for Budget Reports   1987

Marginal Tax Rate   25 %

Investment Report Date   01 / 15 / 87

Include Retirement Plan Assets on
Portfolio   (Y/N) y

Spouse

Name: Sara R. Minor

Birthplace: Boston, Ma.

Birth Date: 09 / 16 / 56

Soc. Sec. # 145 / 46 / 3309

Occupation: Line Mgr.

Emply/Bus: T.I.

Address: 10 West Loop

City: Houston

State: Tx.   ZIP: 77021

Bus. Phone: (714) 459-8601

Retirement Information:

Client's Retirement Age   70

Client's Soc. Sec. %   100 %

Spouse's Retirement Age   62 %

Spouse's Soc. Sec. %   80 %

Growth Rates:

Investment Rate after
Retirement   7 %

Soc. Sec. Benefits Growth Rate   3 %

Educational Costs Growth Rate   4 %

Investment Rate Growth Pre-Ret.   8 %

Inflation Rate Before Retir.   5 %

Inflation Rate After Retir.   5 %

Tax Rate for Educational Funds   16 %

Home Address

Address: 14202 Appleseed

City: Houston   ST: Tx. ZIP: 77041

Home Phone: (714) 862-4903

205

Appendix A

I M P O R T A N T   P A R T I E S

Code# _1___ Name _____Jerry Brown_____

Firm ___Accountant's, Inc._____ Address ____2401 Moon St._____

City ___Houston,_____ State _Tx__ Zip _77041_ Phone _714_/ _883-4026___

===

Code# _4___ Name _____Mike Martin_____

Firm ___Planners, Inc._____ Address _____14101 S.W. Freeway, S124

City ___Houston_____ State _Tx._ Zip _77012_ Phone _714_/ _235-8304___

===

Code# _____ Name _____

Firm _____ Address _____

City _____ State _____ Zip _____ Phone _____/_____

===

Code# _____ Name _____

Firm _____ Address _____

City _____ State _____ Zip _____ Phone _____/_____

===

Code# _____ Name _____

Firm _____ Address _____

City _____ State _____ Zip _____ Phone _____/_____

===

#Code:

1 - Accountant	4 - Financial Planner	7 - Executor of Client's Will
2 - Attorney	5 - Investment Advisor	8 - Executor of Spouse's Will
3 - Banker	6 - Insurance Advisory	9 - Children's Guardian

Appendix A

GOALS AND OBJECTIVES

Code# ___1_____   Goal or Objective (1 Per Screen):

_Save_for_a_lake_house_in_two_years._____

===

Code# __2_____   Goal or Objective (1 Per Screen):

_More_vacation_money._____

_Send_kids_to_college._____

===

Code# __3_____   Goal or Objective (1 Per Screen):

_Invest_in_some_business_interest_by_1990._____

===

Code# __4_____   Goal or Objective (1 Per Screen):

_Invest_for_retirement_indepedence_____

===

Code# __5_____   Goal or Objective (1 Per Screen):

_Leave_enough_money_and_assets_for_the_family_to_continue_financially_.

===

Code# _____   Goal or Objective (1 Per Screen):

===

#Code:
1 - Personal	3 - Financial	5 - Estate Planning
2 - Family	4 - Retirement	6 - Business

207

Appendix A

FINANCIAL STATEMENT INFORMATION

Income		Contingent Liabilities	
Description	Amount	Description	Amount
Salary - Jack	23,400		
Bonus - Jack	1,200		
Salary - Sara	17,500		
Interest - C.D.	1,125		

Are any assets pledged?   (Y/N) __n__

Any past bankruptcy?   (Y/N) __n__

Defendant in any suit?   (Y/N) __n__

Appendix A

M O N E Y   M A R K E T   A S S E T S

ASSET INFORMATION

Bank/Fund: __First National Bank__   Type of Account: __Checking__

Current Balance: __2,000__   Interest Rate: __6__   Maturity: _____

Ownership Code (H/W/J/C/T) __J__   Guaranteed: (Y/N) __N__   Pledged (Y/N) __N__

Money Market Code#: __CS__   Itemize on Page 1 of Financial Statement: (Y/N) __N__

+CS - Checking or Savings
MM - Money Market Mutual Funds
CD - Certificate of Deposit
GS - Government Securities

RETIREMENT ASSUMPTIONS

Accumulate Value of Asset for Retirment Funding (Y/N): __N__

If "Y", then at what rate: __0__

Will this Asset be Included as Part of a Plan Projection (Y/N): __N__

==

ASSET INFORMATION

Bank/Fund: __Houston Federal__   Type of Account: __C.D. 143021 -M__

Current Balance: __15,000__   Interest Rate: __7.50__   Maturity: __10-14-87__

Ownership Code (H/W/J/C/T) __J__   Guaranteed: (Y/N) __Y__   Pledged (Y/N) __N__

Money Market Code#: __CD__   Itemize on Page 1 of Financial Statement: (Y/N) __N__

+CS - Checking or Savings
MM - Money Market Mutual Funds
CD - Certificate of Deposit
GS - Government Securities

RETIREMENT ASSUMPTIONS

Accumulate Value of Asset for Retirment Funding (Y/N): __N__

If "Y", then at what rate: __0__

Will this Asset be Included as Part of a Plan Projection (Y/N): __N__

209

Appendix A

G E N E R A L   A S S E T S

ASSET INFORMATION

Description: _____ Household Furnishings _____

Purchase Price: ___0_____   Purchase Date: _____/_____/_____   Current Value: ___20,000____

Ownership Code: (H/W/J/C/T):J_____   Asset Code:* _____NP_____

Itemize on Page 1 of Financial Statement (Y/N): _____N_____

RETIREMENT ASSUMPTIONS

Accumulate Value of Asset for Retirement Funding (Y/N): _____N_____

If "Y" then at what Rate: _____0_____

Will this Asset be Included as Part of a Plan Projection (Y/N): _____N_____

Description: _____ Pension - Retirement _____

Purchase Price: ___0_____   Purchase Date: _____/_____/_____   Current Value: ___7,000_____

Ownership Code: (H/W/J/C/T):__C_____   Asset Code:* _____RP_____

Itemize on Page 1 of Financial Statement (Y/N): _____N_____

RETIREMENT ASSUMPTIONS

Accumulate Value of Asset for Retirement Funding (Y/N): _____Y_____

If "Y" then at what Rate: _____8_____

Will this Asset be Included as Part of a Plan Projection (Y/N): _____N_____

Description: _____ 1985 Chev. _____

Purchase Price: _____13,200____   Purchase Date: ___09__/___09__/__85__   Current Value: _____11,100____

Ownership Code: (H/W/J/C/T):____J_____   Asset Code:* _____NP_____

Itemize on Page 1 of Financial Statement (Y/N): _____N_____

RETIREMENT ASSUMPTIONS

Accumulate Value of Asset for Retirement Funding (Y/N): _____N_____

If "Y" then at what Rate: _____0_____

Will this Asset be Included as Part of a Plan Projection (Y/N): _____N_____

*ASSET CODES
IP - Tangible Investments   RP - Retirement Plans   TR - Real Estate Partnership
NP - Non-Investment Property   BU - Business Interests   TE - Equipment Leases
AR - Accounts Receivable   TO - Oil & Gas Interests   TX - Other

Appendix A

L I A B I L I T I E S (Non - Real Estate)

Loan Code:* _____ L _____

Description: _____ 1985 - Chev. _____

Creditor: _____ First National Bank _____

Current Balance: _ 7,200 _____ Interest Rate: _____ 12 _____

Payment Amount: _____ 220.00 _____ Payments per Year: _____ 12 ____

Maturity: _____ Ownership Code (H/W/J/C/T): _____ J ____

Pay Liability on Husband's Death (Y/N): _____ Y _____

Pay Liability on Wife's Death (Y/N): _____ Y _____

==

Loan Code:* _____ L _____

Description: _____ Credit Cards _____

Creditor: _____ Various _____

Current Balance: _ 1,500.00 _____ Interest Rate: _____ 18 _____

Payment Amount: _____ 100.00 _____ Payments per Year: _____ 12 ____

Maturity: _____ Ownership Code (H/W/J/C/T): _____ J ____

Pay Liability on Husband's Death (Y/N): _____ Y _____

Pay Liability on Wife's Death (Y/N): _____ Y _____

==

Loan Code:* _____

Description: _____

Creditor: _____

Current Balance: _____ Interest Rate: _____

Payment Amount: _____ Payments per Year: _____

Maturity: _____ Ownership Code (H/W/J/C/T): _____

Pay Liability on Husband's Death (Y/N): _____

Pay Liability on Wife's Death (Y/N): _____
==

   *C - Credit Cards
   L - Secured Loans
   U - Unsecured Loans

211

Appendix A

REAL ESTATE INFORMATION

ASSET INFORMATION

Location: _____ 14292 Appleseed _____   Description: _____ Residence _____

Current Market Value: _ 73,000 _____   Ownership Code (H/W/J/C/T): __ J ____

Real Estate Code: _____ R _____   Itemize on Page 1 of Financial Statement (Y/N): ___ N ___

  *R - Personal Real Estate
  I - Income Property
  U - Undeveloped Real Estate

RETIREMENT ASSUMPTIONS

Accumulate Value of Asset for Retirement Funding (Y/N): _____ Y _____

If "Y", then at what Rate: _____ 8 _____

Will this Asset be Included as Part of a Plan Projection (Y/N): _____ N _____

REAL ESTATE LIABILITIES

Description: _____ 14202 Appleseed _____   Creditor: __ First Mortgage M-23933 ____

AMORTIZATION DATA

Balance Amount: __ 71,300 ____   Balance Mo/Yr _ 01 _/_ 87 ____   Payment Amount: __ 750.00 ____

Interest Rate: __ 10.75 ____   Payments/Year: __ 12 _____   Maturity Date: _____/_____

Current Balance: _ 71,300 ___   Print Report for: __ 2 ____ years   Starting in Year: _ 1987 ___

Pay off upon Husband's Death (Y/N): _____ Y _____   Pay off upon Wife's Death (Y/N): _____ Y _____

Balloon Payment Data   -1-   -2-   -3-   Cash Out

     Date:_____   _____   _____   _____

    Amount: _____   _____   _____   _____

212

Appendix A

H O M E O W N E R S   I N S U R A N C E

Description of Property __Residence__

Address __14202 Appleseed__   Renewal Date: ___07___ / ___12__ / __87___

Policy Form ___HO3___   Company ___Sentry___

Coverage Limits:

Primary Dwelling _____70,000_____   Personal Property ____60,000____

Detached Structures _____0_____   Living Expenses ____25,000____

Annual Premium _____800_____   Deductible Amount ____250____

Riders_____ _____ _____

==

Description of Property _____

Address _____   Renewal Date: _____/_____/_____

Policy Form _____   Company _____

Coverage Limits:

Primary Dwelling _____   Personal Property _____

Detached Structures _____   Living Expenses _____

Annual Premium _____   Deductible Amount _____

Riders_____ _____ _____

==

Description of Property _____

Address _____   Renewal Date: _____/_____/_____

Policy Form _____   Company _____

Coverage Limits:

Primary Dwelling _____   Personal Property _____

Detached Structures _____   Living Expenses _____

Annual Premium _____   Deductible Amount _____

Riders_____ _____ _____

213

Appendix A

A U T O M O B I L E   I N S U R A N C E

Automobile ___1985 Chev._____   Company Name ___Protection Ins._____

Policy Number ___45903 -R_____   Number of Drivers ___20,000_____

Coverage Limits:

　　Personal Injury ___50/100_____   Property Damage ___20,000_____

　　Medical Payments ___30,000_____

Annual Premium _____600_____   Renewal Date: ___05_/__14_/___87_____

Deductible Amounts:　　　　　Collision ___250_____   Comprehensive __50____

Riders _____   _____   _____

==

Automobile_____   Company Name _____

Policy Number _____   Number of Drivers _____

Coverage Limits:

　　Personal Injury _____   Property Damage _____

　　Medical Payments _____

Annual Premium _____   Renewal Date: _____/_____/_____

Deductible Amounts:　　　　　Collision _____   Comprehensive _____

Riders _____   _____   _____

==

Automobile_____   Company Name _____

Policy Number _____   Number of Drivers _____

Coverage Limits:

　　Personal Injury _____   Property Damage _____

　　Medical Payments _____

Annual Premium _____   Renewal Date: _____/_____/_____

Deductible Amounts:　　　　　Collision _____   Comprehensive _____

Riders _____   _____   _____

214

Appendix A

Policy Type _____ Group _____ Company _____ Sentry _____

Primary Insured ___ Jack _____ Dependent Coverage (Y/N) _____ Y _____

Basic Sickness and Accident Coverage

Number of Hospital Days _____ 360 _____ Surgical Coverage _____ Scheduled _____

Deductible Amounts: Per Illness _ 200 ____   Per Year _ 600 _____

Major Medical Coverage

Deductible Amount: _ 250 _____ Co-Insurance _____ 80 __% Maximum Coverage __ 1,000,000 __

Annual Premium Paid By You _____ 0 _____

===

Policy Type _____ Company _____

Primary Insured _____ Dependent Coverage (Y/N) _____

Basic Sickness and Accident Coverage

Number of Hospital Days _____ Surgical Coverage _____

Deductible Amounts: Per Illness _____   Per Year _____

Major Medical Coverage

Deductible Amount: _____ Co-Insurance _____% Maximum Coverage _____

Annual Premium Paid By You _____

===

Policy Type _____ Company _____

Primary Insured _____ Dependent Coverage (Y/N) _____

Basic Sickness and Accident Coverage

Number of Hospital Days _____ Surgical Coverage _____

Deductible Amounts: Per Illness _____   Per Year _____

Major Medical Coverage

Deductible Amount: _____ Co-Insurance _____% Maximum Coverage _____

Annual Premium Paid By You _____

Appendix A

DEPENDENTS/EDUCATION

Name ___Mickey___J._____ Relationship* _____S_____ -___

                                                     *S - Son
                                                     D - Daughter
                                                     O - Other

Birthdate ___12-14-79_____

Birthplace ___Houston, Tx._____ Soc. Sec. #: _____443-21-8305_____

Educational Funding	School #1	School #2
Current Assets	2000	
Current Cost/Yr:	5000	
Number of Years:	4	
% To be Funded	80	

===

Name Patrica_____ Relationship* _____D_____

                                                     *S - Son
                                                     D - Daughter
                                                     O - Other

Birthdate ___02-23-73_____

Birthplace _____Houston, Tx._____ Soc. Sec. #: _____423-83-810_____

Educational Funding	School #1	School #2
Current Assets	2000	
Current Cost/Yr:	5000	
Number of Years:	4	
% To be Funded	80	

===

Appendix A

R E T I R E M E N T   I N C O M E

Income Needed at Retirement (Present Value Dollars): _____2,800_____ per Month.

Retirement Capital to remain at Age ____85____ $ ____200,000____

Fixed Income Sources (Monthly)

DESCRIPTION	AMOUNT AT RETIREMENT	5 YRS AFTER RETIREMENT	10 YRS AFTER RETIREMENT	15 YRS AFTER RETIREMENT	20 YRS AFTER RETIREMENT
Pension	700	700	700	700	700

217

Appendix A

RETIREMENT PLAN PROJECTIONS

Projection for (H/W/J):   H   Type of Projection:*   I.R.A.

                                                   Invested In: First Insurance Company

Beneficiary at Death (H/W/T/O)   W   Investment Growth Rate: 7

Current Balance: 200.00   Alternate Investment Growth Rates:

Current Contribution: 200.00   _____ % from Year # _____ to Year # _____

Contributions Per Year: 1   _____ % from Year # _____ to Year # _____

Beginning/Ending (B/E)   E   _____ % from Year # _____ to Year # _____

Contribution Growth: 0   Projected Inflation Rate: 5

Maximum Contribution: 0   Suspend Contributions at Age: 70

                                                   Continue Projection to Age: 70

*Type of Projection:

IR – IRA
KE – Keogh
PS – Profit Sharing
PE – Pension Plan
TD – TDA/TSA
SP – Savings Plan (may be non-qualified and joint)

218

Appendix A

ESTATE PLAN ASSUMPTION

	Client's Death	Spouse's Death

CURRENT WILL

Type:* _____P_____   Final Expenses _____10000_____ _____10000_____

% Estate to Spouse __50_____%   Administrative Cost _____8_____% _____8_____%

                                      Bequests to Others _____0_____ _____0_____

RECOMMENDED WILL   Unified Credit Used _____0_____ _____0_____

Type:* _____P_____   Emergency Fund _____10000_____ _____10000_____

% Estate to Spouse __100_____%   Educational Fund _____46700_____ _____46700_____

Will Code for Above
*P - Percentage Will   Charitable Bequests _____0_____ _____0_____
T - Tax Credit Will
X - Optimum Marital Ded.   Surv. Spouse Need/Yr _____18000_____ _____18000_____

ASSUMPTIONS

Estate Growth % ____8_____%

Year of First Death ____1987_____

Year of Second Death ____1997_____

Appendix A

DISABILITY NEEDS

Current Annual Living Expenses: ___38,000___ Inflation Rate: ___5___

Percentage of Current Income Needed in Event of Disability: ___80___

Income Source	Year 1	Year 2	Year 3	Year 6+
Sara- Salary	$ 17,500	$ 17,500	$ 18,300	$ 18500
*				

* Program calculates the S.S. automatically.

220

Appendix A

I N C O M E   C A S H / F L O W

Description _____ Jack's Salary _____

	Year 1	Year 2	Year 3
Taxable Income	23,400	25,000	27,000
Cash Flow	21,200	23,500	24,100

Soc. Sec. Code* _____ E   Type* _____   State Tax Code* _____ T
 *E - Employee   *P - Personal Service   *Y - Taxable
  S - Self Employed   N - Non Personal Service   N - Non Taxable
  F - Farm   I - Investment   S - State Tax Only

Ownership (H/W/J) _____ H   Include on Which Reports (P/F) _____
                                  (Leave Blank for Both)

==

Description _____ Sara's Salary _____

	Year 1	Year 2	Year 3
Taxable Income	17,500	17,900	18,400
Cash Flow	17,230	17,290	17,950

Soc. Sec. Code* _____ E   Type* _____   State Tax Code* _____ T
 *E - Employee   *P - Personal Service   *Y - Taxable
  S - Self Employed   N - Non Personal Service   N - Non Taxable
  F - Farm   I - Investment   S - State Tax Only

Ownership (H/W/J) _____ W   Include on Which Reports (P/F) _____
                                  (Leave Blank for Both)

==

Description _____ Houston Federal _____

	Year 1	Year 2	Year 3
Taxable Income	1125	1125	1125
Cash Flow	1125	1125	1125

Soc. Sec. Code* _____   Type* _____ I   State Tax Code* _____ T
 *E - Employee   *P - Personal Service   *Y - Taxable
  S - Self Employed   N - Non Personal Service   N - Non Taxable
  F - Farm   I - Investment   S - State Tax Only

Ownership (H/W/J) _____ J   Include on Which Reports (P/F) _____
                                  (Leave Blank for Both)

==

221

Appendix A

T A X   D E D U C T I O N S

	YEAR 1	YEAR 2	YEAR 3	Applies to State Tax (Y/N/S)	Report (P/F)
MEDICAL					
Medical Ins. Premium	900	1000	1000		
Medicine & Drugs	660	1800	600		
Medical/Dental Expenses					
TAXES					
State & Local Taxes					
Real Estate Taxes	1875	1950	2000		
General Sales Taxes					
INTEREST					
Home Mortgage	7000	6950	6950	Y	

222

Appendix A

Description	Year 1	Amount Year 2	Year 3	Applies To State Tax (Y/N/S)	Report (P/F)
I.R.A. - Sara	800	800	800		
---------------------------	---------------	---------------	---------------	------------	--------
---------------------------	---------------	---------------	---------------	------------	--------
---------------------------	---------------	---------------	---------------	------------	--------
---------------------------	---------------	---------------	---------------	------------	--------
---------------------------	---------------	---------------	---------------	------------	--------
---------------------------	---------------	---------------	---------------	------------	--------
---------------------------	---------------	---------------	---------------	------------	--------
---------------------------	---------------	---------------	---------------	------------	--------
---------------------------	---------------	---------------	---------------	------------	--------
---------------------------	---------------	---------------	---------------	------------	--------
---------------------------	---------------	---------------	---------------	------------	--------
---------------------------	---------------	---------------	---------------	------------	--------

223

Appendix A

EXPENSE INFORMATION

Expense Code:# ___LO_____   Description: ___Various_____

Annual Expenses: Year 1: _32,000_____   Year 2: ____32,000_____   Year 3: _35,000_____

Frequency:## ___M_____   Use for Which Report (P/F): _____

	JANUARY	FEBRUARY	MARCH	APRIL	MAY	JUNE
Projected:	2666	2666	2666	2666	2666	2666
Actual:						

	JULY	AUGUST	SEPTEMBER	OCTOBER	NOVEMBER	DECEMBER
Projected:	2666	2666	2666	2666	2666	2666
Actual:						

==

Expense Code:# _____   Description: _____

Annual Expenses: Year 1: _____   Year 2: _____   Year 3: _____

Frequency:## _____   Use for Which Report (P/F) _____

	JANUARY	FEBRUARY	MARCH	APRIL	MAY	JUNE
Projected:						
Actual:						

	JULY	AUGUST	SEPTEMBER	OCTOBER	NOVEMBER	DECEMBER
Projected:						
Actual:						

==

#Expense Code:

LF - Food	LT - Transportation	IL - Life Insurance	IO - Other Insurance
LC - Clothing	LR - Recreation	IM - Medical Insurance	DC - Consumer Debt
LH - Houston	LO - Other Living	ID - Disability Insurance	DO - Other Debt

==

##FREQUENCY

A - Annual	M - Monthly	I - Irregular
S - SemiAnnual	Q - Quarterly	

224

Appendix A

T A X   P L A N N I N G   R E C O M M E N D A T I O N S

Description of Investment: ___Jack - I.R.A._____   Financial Statement Value: ___2000_____

Year 1	Year 2	Year 3
Investment: ___2000_____	Investment: ___2000_____	Investment: ___2000_____

FEDERAL TAXES

Write-Off: ___100%_____	Write-Off: ___100%_____	Write-Off: ___100%_____
Tax Credit: _____	Tax Credit: _____	Tax Credit: _____
Tax Preference: _____	Tax Preference: _____	Tax Preference: _____

STATE TAXES

Write-Off: _____	Write-Off: _____	Write-Off: _____
Tax Credit: _____	Tax Credit: _____	Tax Credit: _____

==

Description of Investment: ___Sara - I.R.A._____   Financial Statement Value: ___1200_____

Year 1	Year 2	Year 3
Investment: ___1200_____	Investment: ___1200_____	Investment: ___1200_____

FEDERAL TAXES

Write-Off: ___100%___	Write-Off: ___100%___	Write-Off: ___100%_____
Tax Credit: _____	Tax Credit: _____	Tax Credit: _____
Tax Preference: _____	Tax Preference: _____	Tax Preference: _____

STATE TAXES

Write-Off: _____	Write-Off: _____	Write-Off: _____
Tax Credit: _____	Tax Credit: _____	Tax Credit: _____

Appendix A

IMPLEMENTATION SCHEDULE

Code# __2__   Time Frame _____60 Days_____

Implementation Item

Need to set up education fund of $200.00 per month.

_____

===

Code# __3__   Time Frame ____Within 6 months_____

Implementation Item

Begin retirement program and invest $975 per month

to overcome projected deficit.

===

Code# __4__   Time Frame _____30 Days_____

Implementation Item

Revise will.

===

Code# __5__   Time Frame _____30 Days_____

Implementation Item

Jack needs $ 135,000 life insurance.

Sara needs $ 130,000 life insurance.

===

Code# __6__   Time Frame _____30 Days_____

Implementation Item

Jack needs $ 575 per month disability income policy.

===

#1 - Risk Management	4 - Estate Planning	7 - Income Tax Planning
2 - Education Funding	5 - Life Insurance	8 - Investments
3 - Retirement Planning	6 - Disability Insurance	9 - Cash Flow Planning

226

Appendix B

Chapter One Flashbacks

1. Purpose is created by ___desire___ and ___belief___.
2. People buy what they ___want___; but they must be sold on those things they ___need___.
3. Success is always achieved by the ___minority___.
4. Successful agents ___form the habit___ of doing things the mediocre either cannot or will not do.
5. ___Self___-___discipline___ is the magical key for engineering success in selling and in life.
6. Never underestimate the power of ___purpose___. This produces six major benefits:
   a. develops self-reliance, personal initiative, imagination, enthusiasm, self-discipline and concentration of effort
   b. motivates you to budget your time
   c. makes you more alert to opportunities
   d. inspires confidence and attracts favorable attention
   e. opens the way to develop faith
   f. makes you success conscious.
7. There are two "green-time" activities: ___calling___ ___for___ ___appointments___ and ___making___ ___sales___ ___presentations___.
8. More than anything else, your ___attitude___ determines your success in managing time.
9. Believe that the power in your sales presentation always lies in its ___simplicity___.
10. Believe that honest, intelligent ___effort___ is always rewarded.

Chapter Two Flashbacks

1. Selling success is the result of
   a. living one's life in _balance_
   b. building a healthy _self-image_
   c. defining and steadfastly pursuing a series of specific, _realistically high goals_
   d. setting up a _mastermind_ alliance
   e. developing _self-discipline_ and self-management skills
   f. displaying faith and _perseverence_
2. Goal setting gives clarity to your _chief aims_ .
3. Ben Feldman said: "We need goals and deadlines—goals big enough to be _exciting_ and deadlines to make us _run_ ."
4. Goals must be _achievable_ , believable, controllable, and be given _deadlines_ .
5. The starting step in planning your success is _self-assessment_ It's here that you examine your _business_ , your personal life, and your _financial_ picture.
6. As you compile your "Master Dream List," remember your only limitations are _self-imposed_ .
7. A yearly budget shows you the income you must produce—as a _minimum_ .
8. Minimum goals are _committed_ goals. Superior goals are _bonus_ goals.
9. Fixing the action plan requires you to construct a _weekly effort formula_ .
10. Planning encourages _disciplined_ action.

Chapter Three Flashbacks

1. Positioning is defined as getting in front of __decision__ __makers__ and creating __selling__ __climates__ that encourage action on your recommendations.
2. Positioning begins with __making a favorable first impression__.
3. It's important to decide how you want to be __perceived__ by your prospects and clients.
4. __Paying__ __attention__ is identified as a way to consistently increase your production.
5. Prospecting becomes as natural as breathing for you when you consistently __pay__ __attention__ and maintain an __action__ __file__.
6. Telephone success requires you to do three things:
   a. always have a __reason__ for calling.
   b. follow a __prepared__ __script__.
   c. be __brief__.
7. Your approach to the first interview has two objectives:
   a. to make a __favorable__ __impression__ upon your prospect.
   b. to arouse __positive__ __interest__.
8. You'll learn to cope with call-reluctance and to build call-courage when you follow these suggestions:
   a. stay __sold__ on what you are selling.
   b. saturate your mind with "__mental__ __vitamins__."
   c. prepare yourself __technically__.
   d. focus on the __rewards__ __of__ __success__.
   e. remind yourself that most people are __nice__ people.
   f. let prospects key-off of your __attitude__ —never key off of your prospects'.

9. The one thing all of your prospects have in common is the need to be __appreciated__. "Ego food" is a powerful substance to use in building relationships, providing it's __believable__.
10. Research reveals ____you____ are the principal reason the buyer ____buys____, becomes a client, and refers others. In a very real sense, you must play the role of being an " __assistant__ __buyer__."

Chapter Four Flashbacks

1. In making sales, the single most important factor is always your _____ confidence _____ .

2. A planned presentation makes it possible for you to listen and study _____ nonverbals _____ . You become a good "eye-listener."

3. The four essentials of an effective presentation are:
   a. it must _____ capture _____ your prospect's instant and undivided _____ attention _____ .
   b. it must _____ arouse _____ interest by describing owner benefits and their _____ advantages _____ to the prospect.
   c. it must _____ create _____ desire by winning your prospect's _____ confidence _____ .
   d. it must _____ motivate _____ your prospect to take _____ action _____ now.

4. _____ Client _____ understanding _____ is the first secret of closing more and better sales.

5. A "controlled question" in selling is one where the response you'll receive is _____ predictable _____ .

6. An assertive attitude of _____ expectancy _____ coupled with a planned _____ strategy _____ leads to closing effectiveness.

7. Objections provide a clue to your prospect's _____ thought _____ _____ process _____ . Objections give you valuable feedback.

8. When objections surface, you handle them in one of three ways—you _____ ignore _____ , defer, or _____ answer _____ them.

9. There are three basic reasons why a prospect is not sold on your recommendation:
   a. something is not _____ understood _____
   b. something is not _____ believed _____
   c. something is being _____ covered _____ up _____

10. Consultative selling requires you to make _____ creative _____ suggestions and to _____ assist _____ the buyer in making a decision.

Chapter Five Flashbacks

1. Image-building and professionalism are closely allied with keeping business on the books and gaining __referral__ __introductions__ .

2. Persistency of business improves when you
   a. look for ___quality___ prospects
   b. sell on the basis of ___needs___
   c. follow up on the ___second___ premiums
   d. develop the ___service___ point of view.

3. Writing a congratulatory letter adds a ___distinctive___ touch and displays ___professionalism___ .

4. The in-person delivery of the contract accomplishes several things:
   a. ___resells___ the need
   b. ___reminds___ of next premium
   c. sets the stage for ___future___ ___sales___
   d. builds the ___relationship___
   e. gets ___referrals___ .

5. An introduction to a referral carries with it the element of being an ___endorsement___ .

6. Sale no. 6, __Getting Referred Leads__ , makes the sale productive and keeps you on "__the selling track__ ."

7. ___Eighty-five percent___ of your effectiveness is determined by your ability to ___manage___ yourself and your skills in ___meeting___ and ___dealing___ with prospects.

8. "Professional equity" is the degree of ___ownership___ you acquire in your career.

9. You enhance your professional equity in these ways:
   a. build __relationships__
   b. acquire symbols of ___excellence___
   c. stay ___contact___-conscious.

10. You create a professional image in these ways:
    a. project _____ success _____
    b. project professionalism at _____ office _____
    c. examine cards, _____ stationary _____ and brochures
    d. organize _____ mailings _____
    e. write _____ articles _____
    f. schedule _____ speeches _____
    g. conduct _____ seminars _____
    h. target _____ advertising _____ .

Chapter Six Flashbacks

1. An eagle is built to soar into the heavens, but can be __conditioned__ to stay earthbound.
2. Winning in selling means __excelling__ at being yourself. Professionals consistently check their __program__ and critique their __performance__.
3. Simply stated, the Lou Behr philosophy is to
   a. wake up each day __employed__
   b. join the "__seven-o'clock__ club"
   c. meet __three__ new people each day.
   d. complete and study a __progress__ report each week.
4. Honest, __intelligent__ effort is always rewarded.
5. "Staying on top" of your business and selling at your best becomes a matter of focusing on __high-payoff__ activities and measuring your __results__ weekly.
6. To function like a professional agent, display __confidence__ and __enthusiasm__ and let it show in your words and actions.
7. To sell skillfully, keep the emphasis on __owner benefits__.
8. The "constant struggle" is between what you are and what you are capable of becoming. __Compete__ but don't compare!
9. The respect for __quality__ never changes. You gain two important dividends by stamping your work with excellence: you build a __following__ and you have the __satisfaction__ of being a real professional.
10. Monitoring __activity__, measuring __results__, and keeping your personal __standards__ high are the kind of habits that move you to the top—and keep you there!

Chapter Seven Flashbacks

1. The essential factor in the success formula is __persistence__.
2. The first element of persistence is knowing __what__ __you__ __want__.
3. The best way to build your desire is by "__creative__ __visualization__."
4. Organized __plans__, even imperfect ones, encourage persistence.
5. Knowing that your plans are sound and based on __facts__ and __experiences__ will encourage persistence.
6. The Mickey Mantle Theory encourages you to be willing to __fail__ repeatedly in order to achieve your selling goals and reach your potential.
7. Joe Gootter said you can manage your __results__ statistically by demonstrating __persistency__ of effort.
8. According to Dr. George W. Crane, successful people in sales often fail because they choose not to live their lives in __balance__.
9. The five dimensions in your "Cross of Life" are
   a. __professional__
   b. __physical__
   c. __financial__
   d. __personal__
   e. __spiritual__
10. Everything necessary for becoming effective in selling can be __acquired__ and __developed__.

Bibliography

Allen, James. *As a Man Thinketh*. Westwood, NJ: Fleming Revell Company. 1957

Anthony, Robert. *Total Self-Confidence*. New York: Berkley Books.

Bach, George R. *The Inner Enemy*. New York: Berkley Books. 1983

Bates, Ernest Sutherland, ed. *The Bible, Designed to be Read as Living Literature*. New York: Simon & Schuster. 1965

Bell, Jesse Grover. *Here's How by Who's Who*. Lakewood, Ohio: Bell, Inc.

Bettger, Frank. *How I Raised Myself from Failure to Success in Selling*. Englewood Cliffs, NJ: Prentice-Hall. 1949

Brande, Dorothy. *Wake Up and Live!* New York: Cornerstone Library, Simon & Schuster. 1969

Brant, Irving. *The Fourth President: A Life of James Madison*. Indianapolis, IN: Bobbs-Merrill. 1970

Bristol, Claude. *The Magic of Believing*. Englewood Cliffs, NJ: Prentice-Hall. 1948

Burns, David D. *Feeling Good*. New York: New American Library. 1980

Carnegie, Dale. *How to Win Friends and Influence People*. New York: Simon & Schuster. 1964

Chinard, Gilbert. *Honest John Adams*. Magnolia, NY: Peter Smith.1964

——— . *Thomas Jefferson: Apostle of Americanism*. Ann Arbor, MI: University of Michigan Press. 1957 rev. ed.

Clason, George S. *The Richest Man in Babylon*. New York: Haethorn Books. 1955

Conwell, Russell. *Acres of Diamonds*. New York: Harper. 1960

Cooper, Kenneth. *Aerobics*. New York: Evans & Company. 1968

——— . *Running without Fear*. New York: Evans & Company. 1985

Crosby, Philip B. *Quality is Free*. New York: New American Library.

Curtis, Donald. *Your Thoughts can Change Your Life*. Englewood Cliffs, NJ: Prentice-Hall. 1961

Davis, Adelle. *Let's Eat Right to Stay Fit*. New York: Signet Books. 1970

Dible, Donald M. *Build a Better You—Starting Now*. Fairfield, CA: Showcase Publishing Company.

Douglas, Lloyd C. *The Magnificent Obsession*. New York: Pocket Books, Simon & Schuster. 1929

Bibliography

Douglas, Mack. *How to Cultivate the Habit of Succeeding*. Grand Rapids, MI: Zondervan Publishing House. 1986

Dudley, George W. and Shannon Goodson. *The Psychology of Call Reluctance*. Dallas: Behavioral Science Research. 1986

Fenton, Lois. *Dress for Excellence*. New York: Rawson Associates.

Flesch, Rudolph. *How to Write, Speak, and Think More Effectively*. New York: New American Library. 1963

———. *The Art of Clear Thinking*. New York: Harper & Brothers. 1951

———. *The Art of Plain Talk*. New York: Harper & Brothers. 1946

———. *The Art of Readable Writing*. New York: Harper & Brothers. 1976

Flynn, John T. *God's Gold: The Story of Rockefeller and His Times*. Westport, CT: Greenwood Press.

Fosdick, Harry Emerson. *On Being a Real Person*. New York: Harper & Row. 1943

Fox, Emmet. *Power through Constructive Thinking*. New York: Harper & Row. 1940

Franklin, Benjamin. *Autobiography*. New York: Dodd, Mead.

Funk, Wilfred. *The Way to Vocabulary Power*. New York: Funk, Inc. 1946

Gandolfo, Joe. *Ideas Are a Dime a Dozen*. Cincinnati: National Underwriter.

Gardner, John W. *Excellence*. New York: Harper & Row.

———. *Self-Renewal*. New York: Harper & Row. 1965

Getty, J. Paul. *How to be Rich*. New York: Playboy, Simon & Schuster. 1965

Graham, Billy. *The Secret of Happiness*. New York: Pocket Books, Simon & Schuster. 1985

Hansen, Mark Victor. *Dare to Win*. Los Angeles: Medallion Books.

Harris, Thomas. *I'm OK—You're OK*. New York: Harper & Row. 1969

Helmstetter, Shad. *What to Say When You Talk to Yourself*. New York: Pocket Books.

Hendrick, Burton J. *Life of Andrew Carnegie*. New York: Arno Press.

Hill, Napoleon. *Law of Success*. New York: Success Unlimited.

———. *Think and Grow Rich*. New York: Fawcett World.

Ingram, K. C. *Winning Your Way with People*. New York: McGraw-Hill.

James, Muriel and Dorothy Jongeward. *Born to Win*. Reading, MA: Addison Wesley. 1971

Jones, Charles. *Life is Tremendous*. Wheaton, IL: Tyndale House.

Kennedy, John Fitzgerald. *Profiles in Courage*. New York: Harper & Row. 1956

Kinder, Jack, Jr. and Garry D. and Roger Staubach. *Winning Strategies in Selling*. Englewood Cliffs, NJ: Prentice-Hall. 1981

Kissling, Fred. *Sell and Grow Rich*. Lexington, KY: Lexington House. 1966

Leider, Richard J. *The Power of Purpose*. New York: Fawcett Books.

Liebman, Joshua. *Peace of Mind*. New York: Simon & Schuster. 1965

Linn, James W. *Jane Addams: A Biography*. West Point, CT: Greenwood Press. 1968

Loehr, James E. and Peter J. McLaughlin. *Mentally Tough*. New York: Evans & Co.

Mackenzie, Catherine D. *Alexander Graham Bell, the Man Who Contracted Space*. New York: Arno Press.

Maltz, Maxwell. *Psycho-Cybernetics*. Englewood Cliffs, NJ: Prentice-Hall. 1960

Mandino, Og. *The Greatest Salesman in the World*. New York: Bantam Books. 1968

———. *The Greatest Miracle in the World*. New York: Bantam Books. 1985

———. *University of Success*. New York: Bantam Books.

McCay, James. *The Management of Time*. Englewood Cliffs, NJ: Prentice-Hall. 1959

McFarland, Kenneth. *Eloquence in Public Speaking*. Englewood Cliffs, NJ: Prentice-Hall.

Menninger, Karl. *Vital Balance: The Life Process in Mental Health & Illness*. New York: Penguin Books.

———. *Whatever Became of Sin*. New York: Hawthorn Books. 1973

Meyer, Ken. *The Shooters*. Rockville Center, NY: Farnsworth Publishing Company.

Minirth, Frank B. and Paul D. Meier. *Happiness is a Choice*. Grand Rapids, MI: Baker Bookhouse. 1978

Molloy, John T. *Dress for Success*. New York: Warner Books. 1976

———. *How to Work the Competition*. New York: Warner Books.

Morgan, John J. B. and Eving T. Webb. *Making the Most of Your Life*. New York: Arno Press.

Nierenberg, Gerald. *How to Read a Person Like a Book*. New York: Simon & Schuster.

Nightingale, Earl. *Nightingale's Greatest Discovery*. New York: Dodd, Mead. 1987

Nixon, Richard M. *Six Crises*. Garden City, NY: Doubleday. 1962

O'Brien, Father John. *The Faith of Millions*. Huntington, AL: Our Sunday Visitor.

Osborn, Alex. *Your Creative Power*. Totowa, NJ: Scribner's. 1948

Palo, Bert. *Motivation Means Millions*. Indianapolis, IN: R&R Newkirk.

Peale, Norman Vincent. *The Power of Positive Thinking*. New York: Fawcett World. 1956

Rau, Bob. *The Finders*. Chicago: Longmon Publishing.

———. *The Keepers*. Chicago: Longmon Publishing.

Ries, Al and Jack Trout. *Positioning*. New York: Warner Books.

Roosevelt, Franklin D. *Looking Forward*. New York: Da Capo Press. 1933

Roth, Charles. *Secrets of Closing*. Englewood Cliffs, NJ: Prentice-Hall. 1970

———. *Treasury of Selling Secrets*. Englewood Cliffs, NJ: Prentice-Hall.

———. *Winning Personal Recognition*. Englewood Cliffs, NJ: Prentice-Hall. 1954

Sandburg, Carl. *Abraham Lincoln*. New York: Harcourt Brace Janovitch. 1939

Sarnoff, Dorothy. *Speech Can Change Your Life*. Garden City, NJ: Doubleday & Company. 1970

Savage, John. *The Easy Sale*. Cincinnati: National Underwriters.

Schuck, Robert L. *Ten Greatest Salespersons*. New York: Harper & Row. 1978

Schuller, Robert. *Move Ahead with Possibility Thinking*. Garden City, NJ: Doubleday & Company. 1967

_____ . *Self-Love—The Dynamic Force of Success*. New York: Hawthorn Books.

Schwartz, David J. *The Magic of Thinking Big*. New York: Berkley Books. 1976

_____ . *The Magic of Getting What You Want*. New York: Berkley Books. 1984

Sherman, Harold. *How to Foresee and Control Your Future*. New York: Fawcett World Library.

Shields, Walter. *How to Succeed in Life Insurance Selling*. Indianapolis, IN: The Rough Notes Company.

Shook, Robert L. and Herbert M. *The Complete Professional Salesperson*. New York: Barnes and Noble.

Sloma, Richard S. *No-Nonsense Planning*. New York: Free Press. 1984

Smiles, Samuel. *Self-Help*. Levittown, NY: Transatlantic.

Speicher, Paul. *154 Messages*. Chicago: Longmon Publishing.

Stone, W. Clement. *Success through a Positive Mental Attitude*. Englewood Cliffs, NJ: Prentice-Hall.

_____ . *The Success System That Never Fails*. Englewood Cliffs, NJ: Prentice-Hall.

Strain, Lois S. and Gladys W. Hudson. *The Story of Paul J. Meyer*. Hollywood, FL: Frederick Fell Publishers.

Sullivan, Frank. *The Critical Path to Sales Success*. Chicago: Longmon Publishing. 1978

_____ . *The Sullivan Method*. Chicago: Longmon Publishing. 1979

Sweetland, Ben. *I Can*. New York: Cadillac Publishing Company.

Taylor, Harold. *Making Time to Sell*. Toronto, Ontario, Canada: Time Management Consultants, Inc.

Ter Horst, Jerald. *Gerald Ford: Past, Present, Future*.

Todd, John. *Ceiling Unlimited*. Louisville, KY: Insurance Field. 1965

Truman, Harry S. *Memoirs: Year of Decision: Years of Trial and Hope*. Garden City, NJ: Doubleday. 1955

Van Fleet, James. *Power with People*. West Nyack, NY: Parker Publishing Company. 1970

Waitley, Denis. *The Psychology of Winning*. Chicago: Nightingale-Conant, Inc. 1983

Walker, Harold Blake. *Power to Manage Yourself*. New York: Harper & Brothers.

Whitney, Robert. *The New Psychology of Persuasion*. Englewood Cliffs, NJ: Prentice-Hall.

———— Hubin, Thomas, and John D. Murphy. *The New Psychology of Persuasion and Motivation in Selling*. Englewood Cliffs, NJ: Prentice-Hall. 1965

Willard, Bill. *The Motivators*. Chicago: Longmon Publishing. 1977

Willingham, Ron. *Integrity Selling*. Garden City, NJ: Doubleday. 1987

Winkler, John K. *Five and Ten: The Fabulous Life of W. Woolworth*. New York: Arno Press. 1951

Woodson, B. N. *More Power to You*. Chicago: Longmon Publishing. 1951

Wyatt, Wes. *How I Became "Mr. Insurance" in My Community*. St. Louis, MO: Commerce Publishing Company.

Index

Index

Divine discontent, 163-164
Dreams
  examination of, 28, 33
  master dream list, 34
  power of, 33
Dun & Bradstreet, 64

E

Epkins, Joe, 66
Excellence, 192-196
  health factors, 193-194
    guidelines for long life, 194
  peak-performer characteristics,
    193
  personal life and, 195-196
  spiritual life and, 196

F

Faith, 6
Feelings of client, uncovering, 82,
  83
Feldman, Ben, 62
Ferns, Tom, 61
Financial self-assessment, 32
First interview, 78-91
  action-producing statement, 86,
    89
  buyer's motives, understanding,
    93, 95-96
  feelings of client, uncovering, 82,
    83
  good first impression, 78-79
    impression builders, 79
  money commitment
    obtaining, 89-91
    strengthening commitment,
      90-91
  need recognition, developing,
    80-82

  preparing prospect, letter for,
    91-93

probing questions
  example of use, 84-86
  improving, 82, 84
  proven questions, 87
  strategic business interview
    questions, 88
  recording data, 89
  trust building, 79-80
  strategies for, 79-80
Fox, Terry, 6-7

G

Galbraith, John W., 192
Goal setting, 26-28
  direction/focus in, 27
  and financial budget, 33, 35
  goal-attainment insurance, 42
  guidelines for, 27
  recognizing goals, 1-2
  and self-suggestion, 1
  types of goals
    minimum goals, 38
    superior goals, 38
  well-conceived goals compared to
    poorly defined goals, 29
  yearly goals, 33
Gootter, Joe, 189
Gray, Albert E.N., 10, 176
Greatest Miracle in the World, The
  (Mandino), 17
Growth trends, evaluating, 23

H

Habits, 23
  forming/altering, 10
  and persistence, 187
Haggai, Tom, 198
Harker, Prudence A., 88
Health, and performance, 193-194
Helmstetter, Dr. Shad, 33

Purpose—*continued*
  definition-of-purpose principle—
    continued
    and sales, 8, 15
    and persistence, 186

Q

Questioning
  Socratic method, 57
  technique for, 57
  use in, 56-57
  See also Probing questions

R

Raymond, Paul, 21
Reece, Bob, 147
Reed, Dick, 48
Referrals
  approach for developing, 147,
    150-151
  client referrals, and prospecting,
    63
  personal stationary approach,
    151, 152
Reputation, 192
  image, creation of, 60
Resistance
  client, dealing with, 73
  sales resistance, 120
  See also Opposition of client.
Rice, Homer, 33
Rosenow, Dr. Edward, 7
Ross, Dr. Irwin, 78

S

Sales
  call courage in, 66-67
  client-building process, 69-70,
    71-72

client resistance to, 72-73
and expectations of salesperson,
  65
making friends and, 64-65
mind-conditioning and, 54-57
  conditioning mind, 54-55
  conditioning subconscious,
    55
"nests" of people, 64
new psychology of, 69
"pledge" for effectiveness, 67
post-sale letter, 144, 146
questioning
  Socratic method, 57
  technique for, 57
  use in, 56-57
sale, definition of, 69
self-confidence in, 66
telephone script, 72
Sales interviews
  ASKS strategy, 111-114
    attract attention, 111
    know you're understood,
      112-114
    stimulate interest, 111-112
    summarize plan, 114
  closing sale, 114-118
    power of words in, 117-118,
      119
    steps in, 114-117
  design factors, 108
  motivational stories, 126-129
  objections
    anticipation of, 106
    genuineness of, 120
    initial resistance, 120
    last-minute objections, 123
    most frequently encountered,
      129-132
    right attitude about, 118
    strategy for dealing with,
      121-123